ADMINISTRATIVE LAW

ADMINISTRATIVE LAW

Sixth Edition

Jack M. Beermann
Philip S. Beck Professor of Law, Boston University School of Law

The *Emanuel CrunchTime*® Series

ASPEN
PUBLISHING

To contact Customer Service, e-mail customer.service@aspenpublishing.com, call 1-800-950-5259, or mail correspondence to:

Aspen Publishing
Attn: Order Department
1 Wall Street
Burlington, MA 01803

1 2 3 4 5 6 7 8 9 0

ISBN 979-8-8941-0475-1

ABOUT ASPEN PUBLISHING

Aspen Publishing is a leading provider of legal education content and digital learning solutions in the United States and globally. Our innovative products and platforms—designed based on best practices in learning science—engage students and enhance outcomes. From textbooks and audiobooks authored by renowned experts to digital platforms and products like LEAF, Connected eBooks, Connected Quizzing, PracticePerfect, and JD-Next, we empower the next generation of legal professionals with innovative, trusted, and accessible resources.

The Aspen Casebook Series, affectionately known as the "red and black" casebooks among law faculty and students, includes hundreds of highly regarded textbooks across more than 80 disciplines. These range from foundational courses like Torts and Contracts to emerging electives such as Sustainability and the Law of Policing. Our study aids, including the popular *Examples & Explanations* series, help law students master complex topics with clarity and confidence.

Aspen's expertise extends to undergraduate education with our Paralegal, Criminal Justice, and Business Law series, offering the same hallmark quality to a broader audience. JD-Next, our groundbreaking online law school prep course and admissions test, provides a realistic preview of law school, equips students with essential skills for academic success, and evaluates their readiness for legal studies.

Aspen Publishing Is Proud to Be a UWorld Company

Since 2003, UWorld has been a global leader in developing high-quality learning tools for students preparing for high-stakes exams. With a commitment to excellence, UWorld has helped millions of students in undergraduate, graduate, and professional programs in fields such as medicine, nursing, finance, and law achieve their academic and career goals.

Founded by Chandra S. Pemmasani, M.D., during his medical residency, UWorld began focusing on medical education and has since expanded into various academic fields, including law. In 2020, UWorld launched its Legal vertical, starting with its comprehensive Multistate Bar Exam (MBE®) Question Bank, followed by the acquisition of Themis Bar Review, which integrated resources to provide a complete bar exam preparation experience. In 2024, UWorld expanded its offerings by acquiring Aspen Publishing, enhancing its suite of legal education products.

Today, UWorld offers an unparalleled range of study materials that blend active learning methods with expert content, ensuring students and educators can access the most effective resources. From bar preparation to law school success, UWorld is committed to supporting the next generation of legal professionals. Learn more at uworld.com.

To the memory of Arthur H. Beermann, the senior partner in the family firm

Summary of Contents

Contents

FLOWCHARTS

CAPSULE SUMMARY

EXAM TIPS

Preface

Thank you for buying this book.

The *CrunchTime* series is intended for people who want Emanuel quality but don't have the time to use the full-length *Emanuel Law Outline* on a subject. We've designed the series to be used in the last few weeks (or even less) before your final exams.

This book includes the following features, most of which have been extracted from the corresponding *Emanuel Law Outline*:

- ***Flowcharts:*** We've reduced many of the principles of administrative law to a series of 12 flowcharts, created specially for this book and never published elsewhere. We think these will be especially useful on open-book exams. The flowcharts begin on page 1.
- ***Capsule Summary:*** This is a 30-page or so summary of the subject. We've carefully crafted it to cover the things you're most likely to be asked on an exam. The Capsule Summary starts on page 39.
- ***Exam Tips:*** We've compiled these by reviewing dozens of actual essay and multiple-choice questions asked in past law-school and bar exams, extracting the issues and "tricks" that surface most often on exams. The Exam Tips start on page 77.
- ***Essay Exam Questions and Answers:*** These questions are actual ones asked on law-school exams. They start on page 99.
- ***Short-Answer Questions and Answers:*** These questions are generally in a yes-or-no format, with a mini-essay explaining each one. The questions start on page 125.
- ***Multiple-Choice Questions and Answers:*** These questions will help you quickly test your knowledge of some basic principles. The questions begin on page 157.

We hope you find this book helpful and instructive.

Good luck.

Jack M. Beermann
Boston, Massachusetts
June 2025
beermann@bu.edu

FLOWCHARTS

FLOWCHARTS

SUMMARY OF CONTENTS

FIGURE 1

APPOINTMENT OF ADMINISTRATIVE OFFICIALS

Use this chart to analyze the constitutionality of the appointment of federal officials.

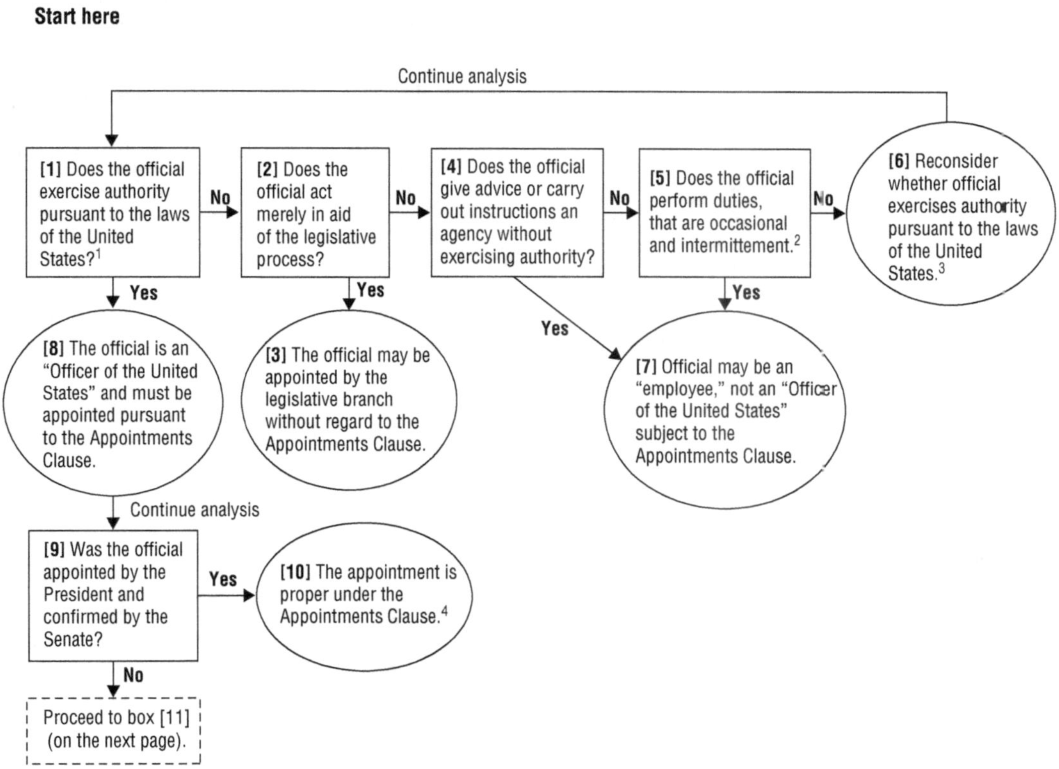

continues on next page

See footnotes after final page of chart

FIGURE 1 (*cont.*)

APPOINTMENT OF ADMINISTRATIVE OFFICIALS

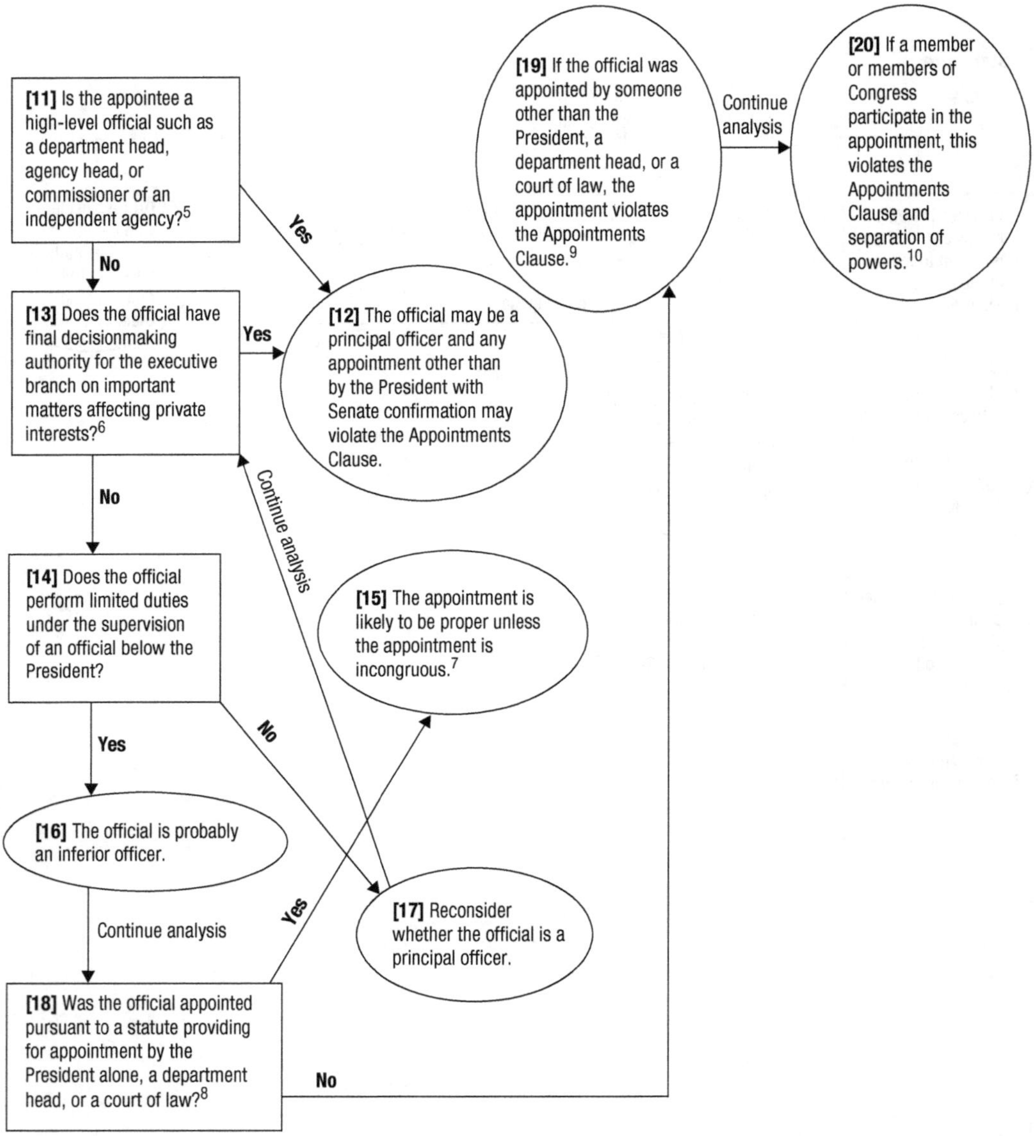

Notes to Figure 1

APPOINTMENT OF ADMINISTRATIVE OFFICIALS

1 This is the standard for determining whether an official is an "Officer of the United States" who may be appointed only pursuant to the Appointments Clause. *See Buckley v. Valeo*, 424 U.S. 1 (1976).

2 In *United States v. Germaine*, 99 U.S. 508 (1878), the Court held that surgeons hired by federal pension commissioners to examine pension applicants and conduct periodic examinations of pension recipients were not "officers of the United States" because they were employed only when needed and were paid by the examination rather than with a regular salary. The Court also noted that the surgeons did not occupy positions established by law; instead, the commissioners themselves determined that their assistance was necessary.

3 There are two categories of federal officials to whom the Appointments Clause does not apply: those acting merely in aid of the legislative process (who may be appointed by Congress or a subset of its members) and those who have no actual authority but rather are merely government "employees." A federal official not in one of those two categories is probably an Officer of the United States to whom the Appointments Clause applies.

4 Absent legislation to the contrary, the model in the Appointments Clause for appointing all Officers of the United States is appointment by the President and confirmation by the Senate. *See* U.S. Const., Art. II, §2, cl. 2.

5 High-level officials such as department heads and independent agency commissioners are "principal" or "superior" officers, and they must be appointed by the President with Senate confirmation. If an official has limited responsibilities and is under the supervision of an executive branch official below the President, the official is probably an inferior officer for whom the Appointments Clause allows an alternative method of appointment. *See Morrison v. Olson*, 487 U S. 654 (1988); *Edmond v. United States*, 520 U.S. 651 (1997).

6 United States v. Arthrex, Inc., 594 U.S. 1 (2021).

7 The Supreme Court has stated that a statute providing for the appointment of an inferior officer by someone other than the President or that officer's department head may be void if there is incongruity between the identity of the appointing official and the duties of the appointee—for example, if Congress designates the Secretary of the Interior as the official with authority to appoint Assistant United States Attorneys.

8 The Appointments Clause allows Congress to specify by statute that inferior officers may be appointed by the President alone, by a department head, or by a court of law. In the absence of such a statute, presidential appointment with Senate confirmation is required.

9 Only those officials named in the Appointments Clause may participate in the appointment of inferior officers.

10 As a corollary to the note above, because Congress or any subset of Congress is not named in the Appointments Clause, a member or members of Congress may not participate in the appointment of inferior officers. In addition, it probably would violate separation of powers for Congress to participate in the appointment of executive branch officials.

Figure 2

REMOVAL OF EXECUTIVE OFFICIALS

Use this chart to analyze whether restrictions on the removal of officers of the United States are constitutional.

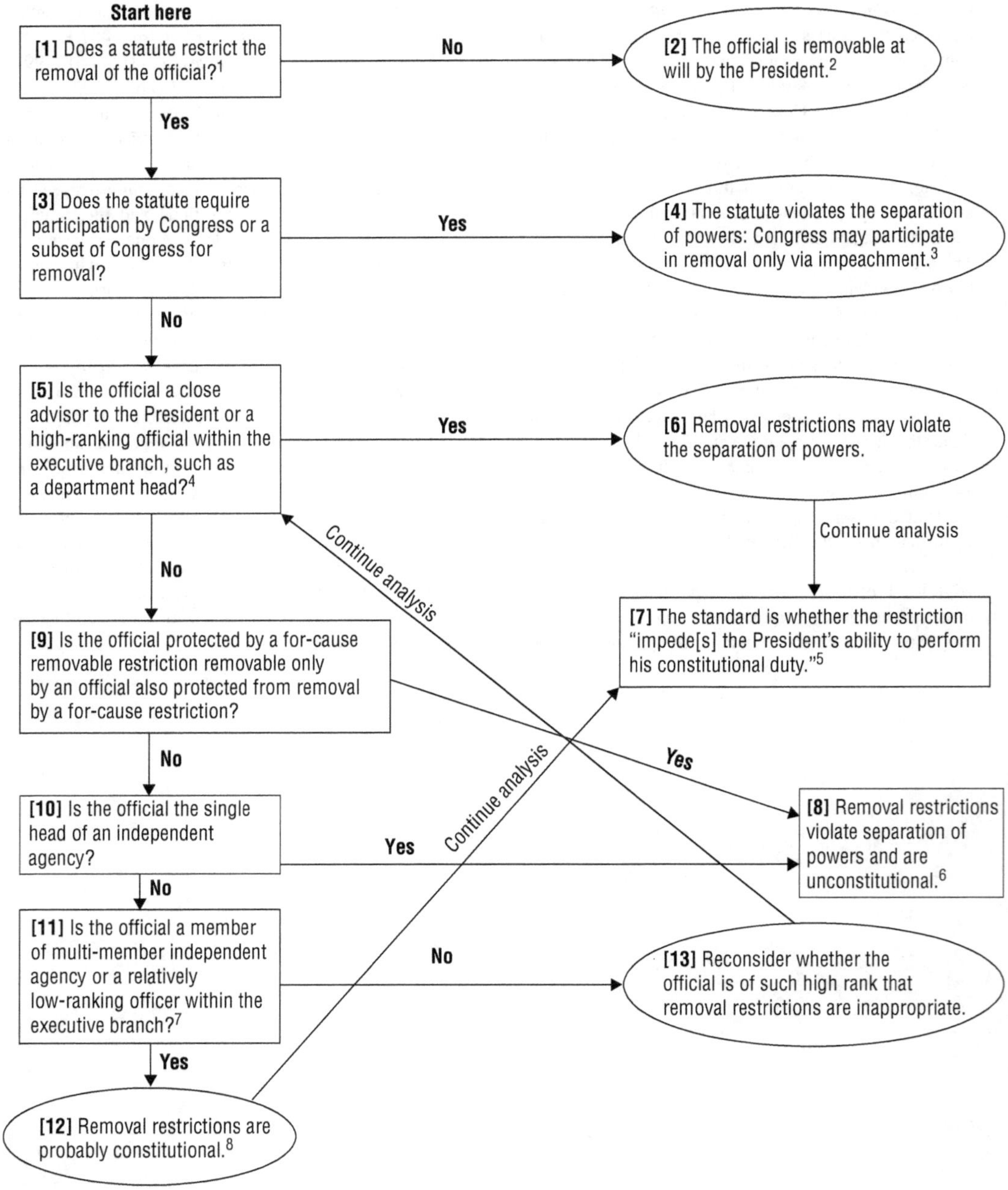

Notes to Figure 2

REMOVAL OF EXECUTIVE OFFICIALS

1 The typical removal restriction provides that an official may not be removed except for good cause. Good cause is often defined as "inefficiency, neglect of duty or malfeasance in office." Some officials are appointed for a term of years and are subject to removal for cause or when their terms expire.

2 There may be nonseparation of powers limits on the ability to discharge officials, such as First Amendment concerns. These are not considered in this chart. Also, the situation of low-level civil service employees is not considered here, only officials considered "Officers of the United States."

3 *Myers v. United States*, 272 U.S. 52 (1926).

4 This question roughly describes the category of officials known as principal or superior officers.

5 *Morrison v. Olson.* The standard announced in *Morrison* repudiates the Court's view in *Humphrey's Executor v. United States*, 295 U.S. 602 (1935), that removal restrictions were justified only when the official performed quasi-legislative and quasi-judicial functions. It does not repudiate the conclusion in *Humphrey's Executor* that the President's power to remove the heads of independent agencies may be restricted by statute. Double for-cause restrictions were held to unduly impede presidential authority in *Free Enterprise Fund v. Public Company Accounting Oversight Board*, 561 U.S. 477 (2009).

6 Seila Law LLC v. Consumer Financial Protection Bureau, 591 U.S. 197 (2020).

7 Officers of the United States who are under the supervision of officials below the President and whose duties are limited are "inferior officers" under the Appointments Clause. Removal restrictions regarding such officials are likely, after *Morrison*, to be upheld.

8 The Court in *Morrison* did allow for the possibility, harkening back to *Humphrey's Executor* and *Myers*, that restrictions on removing officials performing purely executive functions may be unconstitutional, but in *Morrison* itself, the Court upheld restrictions on the removal of a prosecutor, the purest of executive functions.

FIGURE 3

AVAILABILITY OF JUDICIAL REVIEW

Use this chart to determine whether an agency action is reviewable.

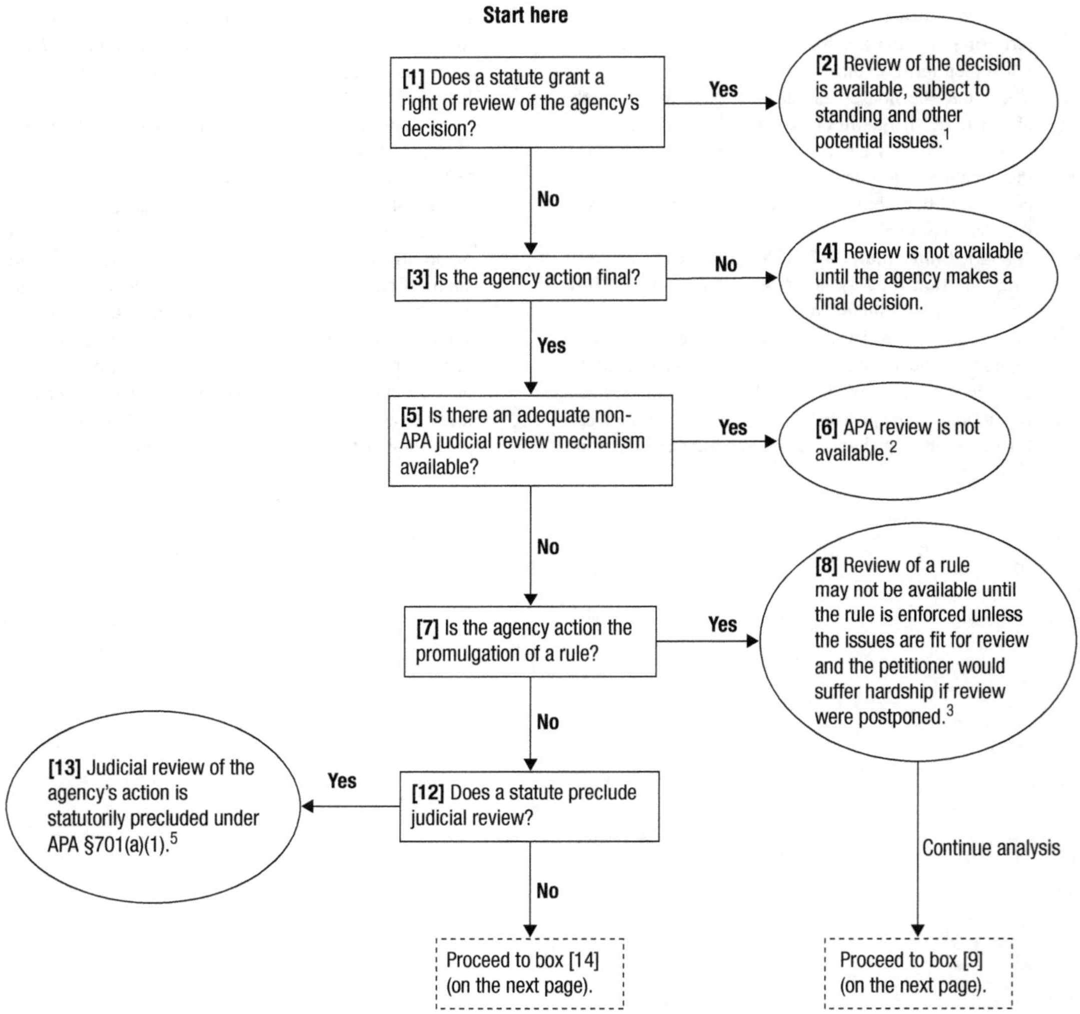

continues on next page *See footnotes after final page of chart*

FIGURE 3 (*cont.*)

AVAILABILITY OF JUDICIAL REVIEW

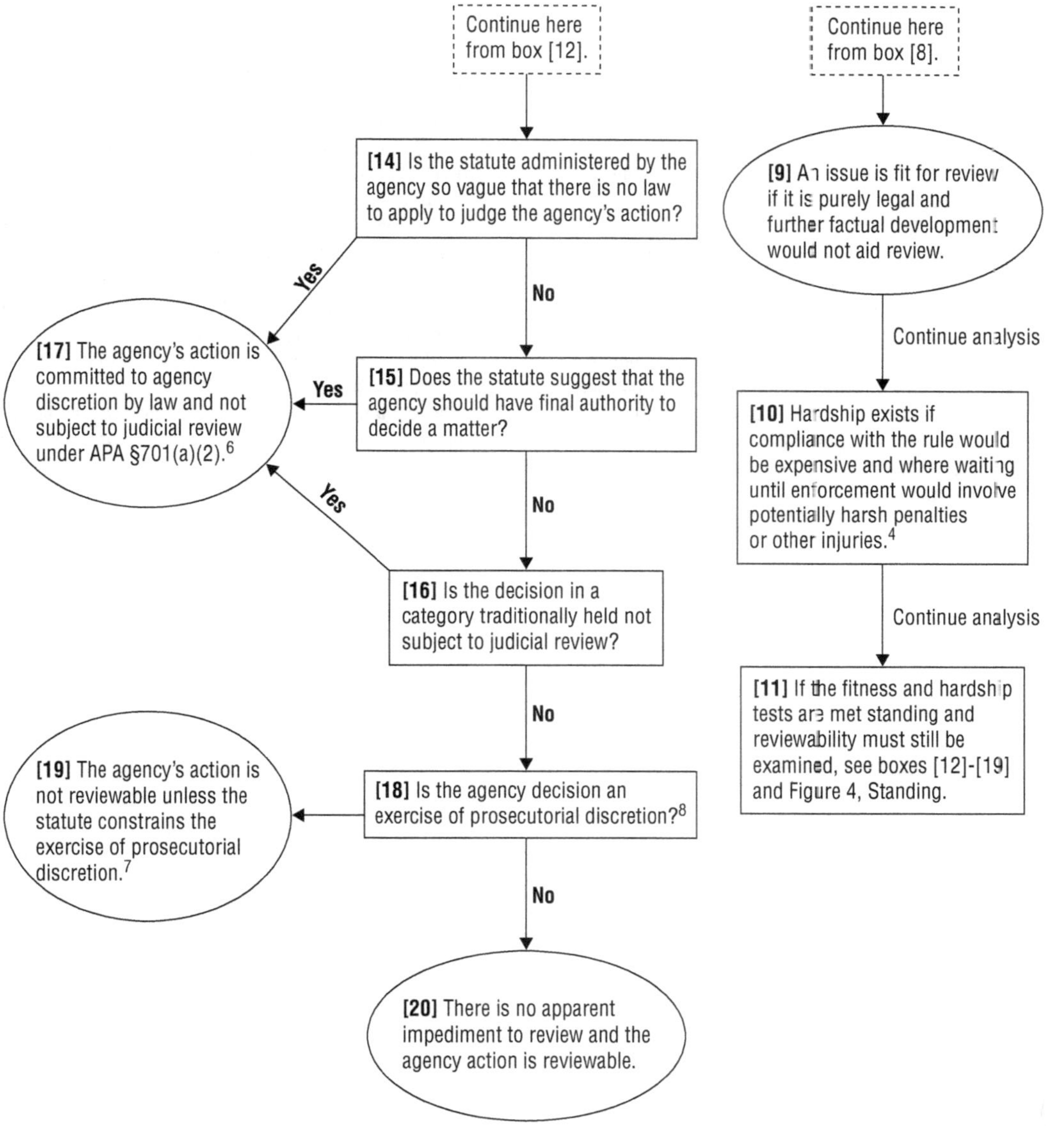

Notes to Figure 3

AVAILABILITY OF JUDICIAL REVIEW

[1] APA §704 states that "agency action made reviewable by statute" is reviewable.

[2] APA §704 states that "final agency action for which there is no adequate remedy in a court" is reviewable.

[3] *See Abbott Laboratories v. Gardner*, 387 U.S. 136 (1967).

[4] *Id.*

[5] For a statute to preclude judicial review, it must mention judicial review and either preclude it altogether or channel review to a method of review different from the one being sought in the case under consideration. For example, the statute in *McNary v. Haitian Refugee Center, Inc.*, 498 U.S. 479 (1991), channeled review of the denial of a special immigrant worker status to review of orders of deportation, thus precluding any other form of review of the denial of the special status. Note also that in the *McNary* case, the Court held that the preclusion of review of individual denials did not preclude review of a general challenge to the administration of the program.

[6] *See Citizens to Preserve Overton Park, Inc. v. Volpe*, 401 U.S. 402 (1971). *Overton Park* stated that agency action was committed to agency discretion by law when there was "no law to apply." The Supreme Court later expanded the definition of "committed to agency discretion by law" to include statutory language indicating that the agency has final authority in *Webster v. Doe*. In *Lincoln v. Vigil*, 508 U.S. 182 (1993), the Court made a further expansion, recognizing that some agency actions are "committed to agency discretion by law" because they are in a category of agency action in which review has traditionally been unavailable. These include prosecutorial discretion and allocation of funds from a lump sum appropriation.

[7] *See Heckler v. Chaney*, 470 U.S. 821 (1985); *Dunlop v. Bachowski*, 421 U.S. 560 (1975).

[8] The denial of a petition requesting that an agency engage in rulemaking is reviewable. *See Massachusetts v. EPA*, 549 U.S. 497 (2007).

FIGURE 4

STANDING

Use this chart to analyze whether a particular plaintiff has standing.

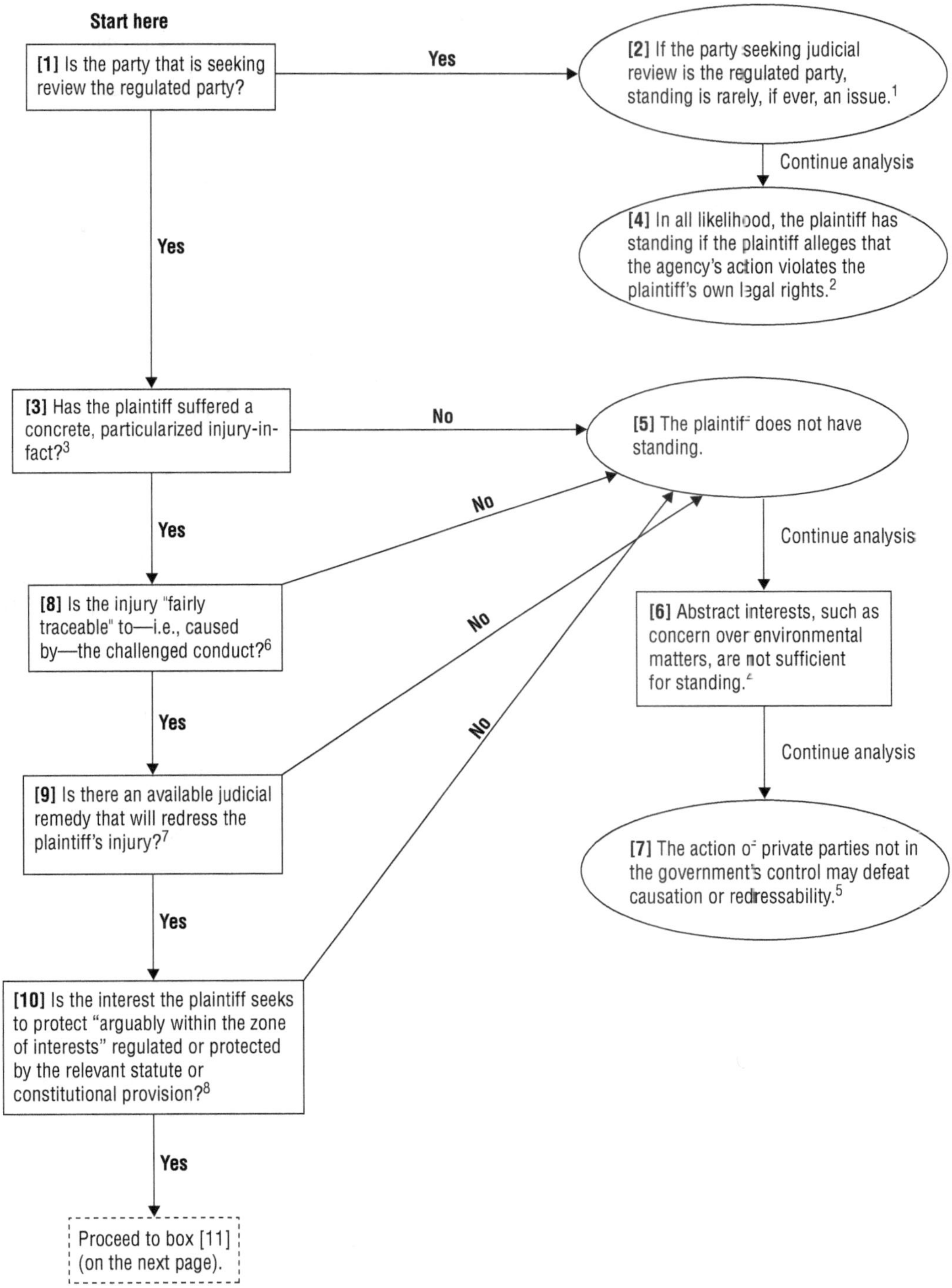

continues on next page

See footnotes after final page of chart

Figure 4 (*cont.*)

STANDING

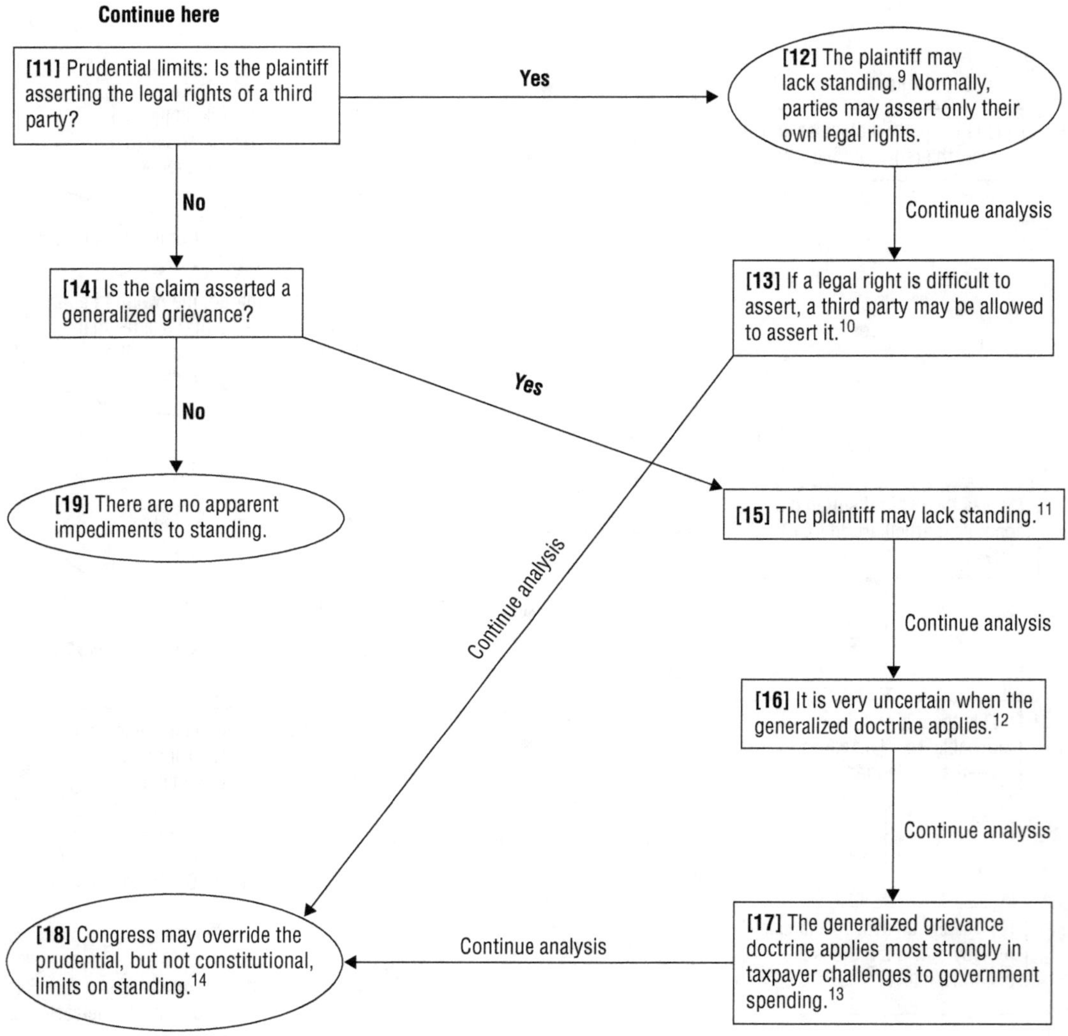

Notes to Figure 4

STANDING

1 The traditional test for standing required that the plaintiff be asserting his or her own legal right against the challenged government action. *Association of Data Processing Service Organizations, Inc. v. Camp*, 397 U.S. 150 (1970), expanded standing beyond these limits but did not affect the standing of those within the traditional core.

2 APA §702 provides standing to "a person suffering legal wrong because of agency action." Standing is rarely an issue if an agency has violated the plaintiff's own legal rights.

3 The authoritative statement of constitutional standing requirements is *Lujan v. Defenders of Wildlife*, 504 U.S. 555 (1992). The basic standing requirements (injury, causation, and redressability) are all stated and analyzed in that case.

4 *See Sierra Club v. Morton*, 405 U.S. 727 (1972); *Lujan v. Defenders of Wildlife.*

5 *See Simon v. Eastern Kentucky Welfare Rights Organization, Inc.* (*EKWRO*), 426 U.S. 26 (1976). In that case, the plaintiffs were injured by the refusal of private hospitals to provide free care. They claimed that this was caused by the IRS's lenient application of standards for hospitals to achieve tax-exempt charitable status. The Court found that the plaintiffs' inability to receive care was caused primarily by the actions of the hospital, not the government, and even if the IRS tightened up its standards, the hospitals might still refuse to provide care.

6 In addition to *Lujan*, cited in note 3, *see United States v. Students Challenging Regulatory Agency Procedures* (*SCRAP*), 412 U.S. 669 (1973), and *Simon v. EKWRO* for analysis of traceability or causation problems in standing.

7 *See EKWRO* and *Lujan* for discussions of redressability.

8 *See Association of Data Processing Service Organizations, Inc. v. Camp*, 397 U.S. 150 (1970); *Air Courier Conference of America v. American Postal Workers Union*, 498 U.S. 517 (1991). The zone of interests test is an interpretation of APA §702, which grants standing to seek judicial review to parties "adversely affected or aggrieved within the meaning of a relevant statute." It may not apply in non-APA cases such as constitutional challenges to agency action.

9 Normally, a party must assert its own legal rights, not the rights of third parties. For example, a store owner cannot assert the rights of her customers to continue receiving food stamps even if the customers' loss of food stamps would injure the store owner by reducing her business. On the other hand, the store owner has standing to assert her own right to accept food stamps at the store.

10 For example, health-care providers have been allowed to litigate their patients' rights to receive abortions on the ground that the patients may find it embarrassing to litigate, and also the patients' claims are transitory.

11 The generalized grievance doctrine is founded on separation of powers concerns and holds that the political branches and not courts are the appropriate forum to resolve controversies that affect many people to a small degree where the plaintiff is not specially affected.

12 In *SCRAP*, the Court stated that the fact that many people are injured by government action should not prevent standing. The plaintiffs in *SCRAP* were injured by increased litter and air and water pollution, and only to a very small extent each. This decision seems to undercut the generalized grievance doctrine.

13 The Court's paradigm case of a generalized grievance is a claim by taxpayers that they are injured when they have to pay taxes to support illegal government programs. However, the Court has allowed taxpayers to challenge legislative (but not administrative) subsidies to religion under the Establishment Clause. *See Flast v. Cohen*, 392 U.S. 83 (1968).

14 In many statutes, especially environmental laws, Congress grants all persons or all citizens the right to challenge specified government action. These statutes override the prudential limits on standing and the zone of interests test. However, the plaintiffs must still establish that they meet the constitutional requirements for standing.

Figure 5

STANDARDS OF JUDICIAL REVIEW OF AGENCY ACTION

Use this chart to choose and apply the correct standard of review of agency action.

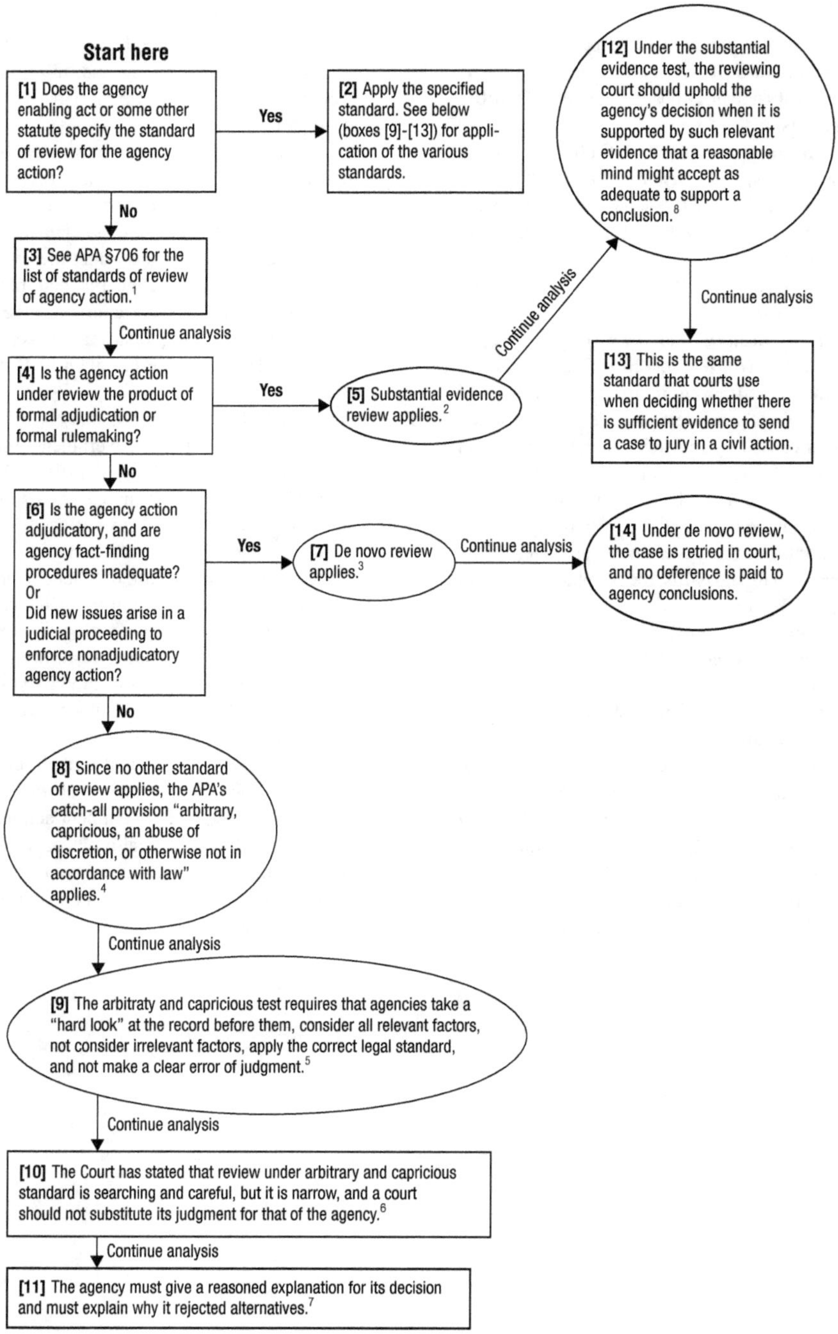

Notes of Figure 5

STANDARDS OF JUDICIAL REVIEW OF AGENCY ACTION

1 This chart looks mainly at APA §706(2)(A), (E), and (F). Other subsections provide that agency action should be set aside if it violates constitutional rights (§706(2)(B)), in excess of statutory jurisdiction (§706(2)(C)) and without observance of proper procedure (§706(2)(D)). Those sections are rarely applied, and they will not be addressed here.

2 *See* APA §706(2)(E), specifying that the substantial evidence test applies in cases when the APA's formal adjudication provisions were applied or where agency action is "reviewed on the record of an agency hearing provided by statute." This final phrase is interpreted to denote formal procedures.

3 The APA does not specify when de novo review applies, but the APA's legislative history clearly points toward application of the pre-APA understanding embodied in box [6] of the chart.

4 APA §706(2)(A), which states the arbitrary and capricious test, contains no restriction on when it applies. Thus, it applies to all reviewable agency action. Because it is the most deferential standard of review in §706, those challenging agency action always prefer one of the other, less deferential standards.

5 In *Massachusetts v. EPA*, the Court clarified that the range of relevant factors is determined with reference to the statute governing agency action. The agency may consider only those factors made relevant by Congress in the governing statute.

6 *Citizens to Preserve Overton Park, Inc. v. Volpe.*

7 *Id.*

8 *See Universal Camera Corp. v. NLRB*, 340 U.S. 474 (1951).

FIGURE 6

CHOICE OF AGENCY PROCEDURE

Use this chart to determine whether an agency is required to use rulemaking or adjudication, or has a choice.

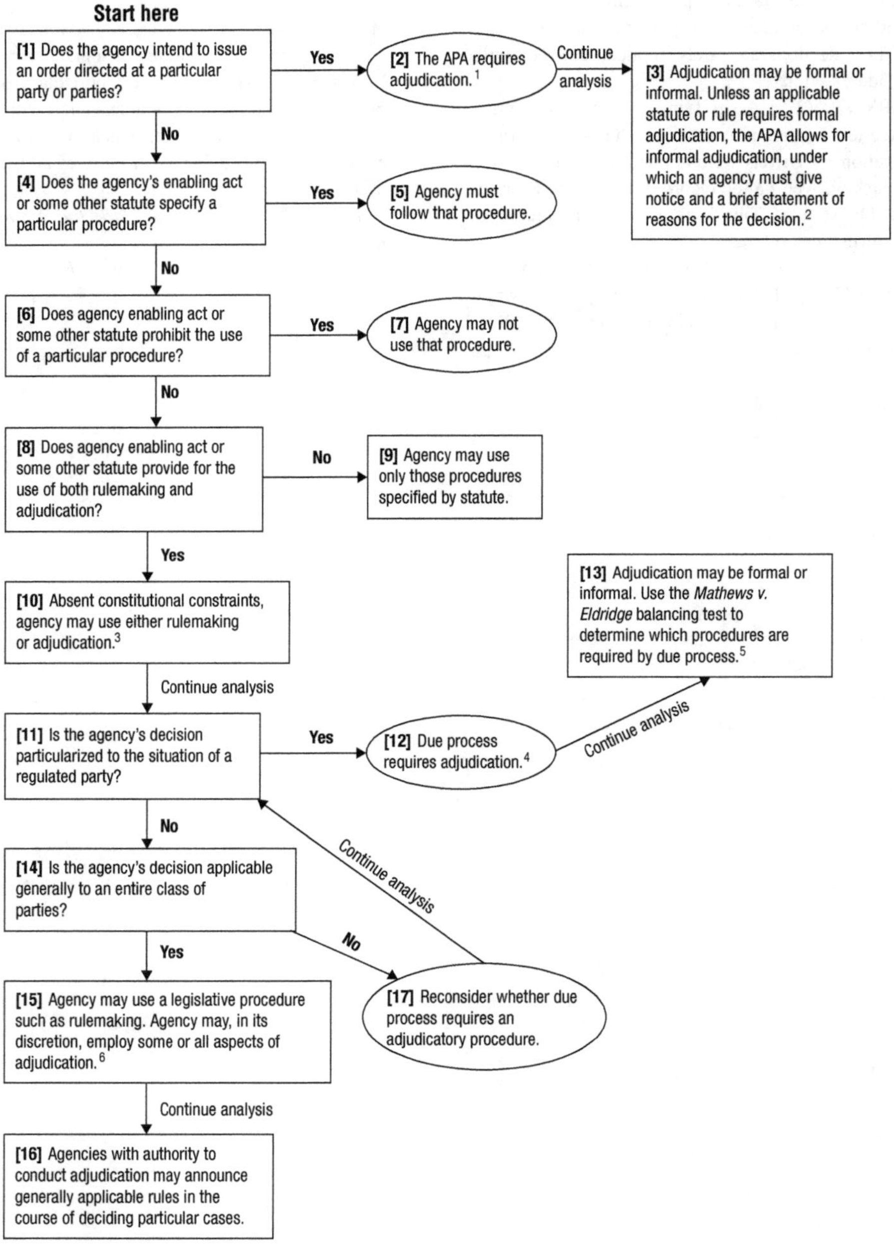

Notes to Figure 6

CHOICE OF AGENCY PROCEDURE

1 5 U.S.C. §551(7) defines "adjudication" as "agency process for the formulation of an order."

2 *See* APA §555(e).

3 Given a choice, agencies usually will choose a legislative procedure such as rulemaking because it is a simpler, less complex procedure. Courts also have recognized that rulemaking has certain policy advantages over adjudication, such as allowing more participation and more comprehensive decision-making, and because of these advantages, courts have liberally construed agency enabling acts and other statutes to allow agencies to use rulemaking.

4 *See Londoner v. Denver*, 210 U.S. 373 (1908). Note that before due process applies, a party must have a protected interest, usually either liberty or property, at stake. When an agency is taking adverse action against a party, for example, by imposing a penalty or antipollution requirements, there is no question that property or liberty is at stake. However, in some cases, such as termination of government employment or government benefits, there may be a question whether liberty or property is present. For property to be involved, a statute, regulation, or entrenched understanding must provide standards against which government action is judged, such as a for-cause standard for termination of employment or a wealth test for benefits. *See Board of Regents v. Roth*, 408 U.S. 564 (1972). Liberty interests, on the other hand, are created by the Constitution itself. Freedom of movement, the ability to practice one's profession, and freedom from physical injury are among the liberties protected by the due process clauses from adverse government action

5 Even when due process under *Londoner* requires an adjudicatory hearing, formal adjudication is not necessarily required. Rather, the *Mathews v. Eldridge*, 424 U.S. 319 (1976), balancing test is used to determine what procedures are required by due process. Under that test, the court considers the strength of the regulated party's interest, the likelihood that additional procedure will produce more accurate results, and the government's interest in minimizing process. When the regulated party's interests are relatively weak and existing procedures already produce a high degree of accuracy, due process may not require more than an informal adjudicatory procedure. On the other hand, when the regulated party's interests are relatively strong, such as the interest in subsistence welfare payments, and existing procedures produce a high likelihood of error, due process may require relatively formal procedures before the government can take even temporary adverse action. See also Figure 9, Due Process and Adjudication.

6 *See Bi-Metallic Investment Co. v. State Board of Equalization*, 239 U.S. 441 (1915).

FIGURE 7

INFORMAL RULEMAKING PROCEDURES

Use this chart to review the procedural requirements for "notice and comment" or informal rulemaking.

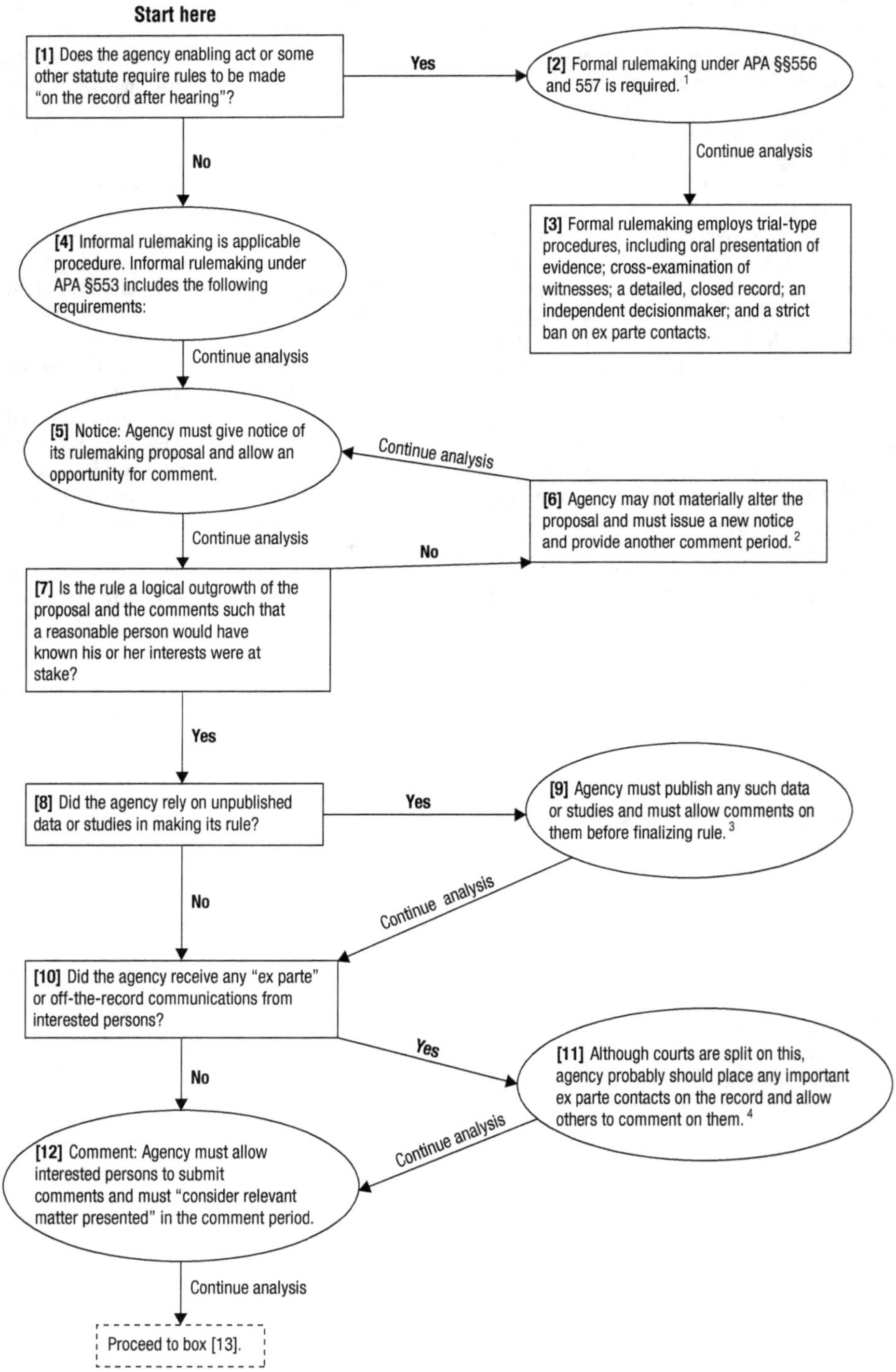

continues on next page

See footnotes after final page of chart

FIGURE 7 (*cont.*)

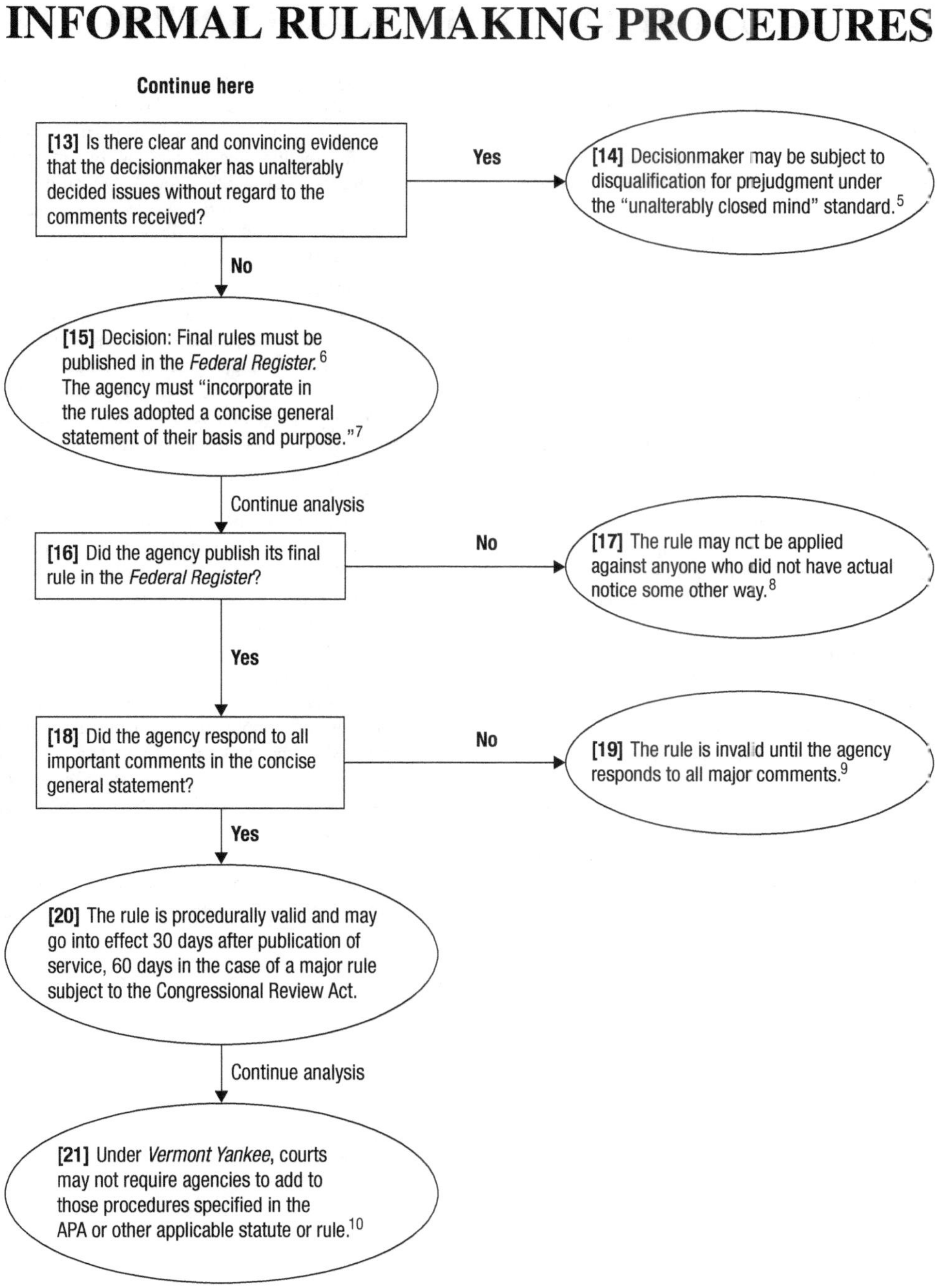

Notes to Figure 7

INFORMAL RULEMAKING PROCEDURES

1 *See* APA §553(c), which states that "when rules are required by statute to be made on the record after opportunity for an agency hearing, sections 556 and 557 of this title apply instead of this subsection." Sections 556 and 557 contain formal adjudicatory procedures. Because formal rulemaking is expensive and time-consuming, agencies rarely use it, and courts do not require agencies to use it unless a statute clearly requires it.

2 APA §553(b)(3) requires notice of the "terms or substance of the proposed rule or a description of the subjects and issues involved." When the final rule differs significantly from the original proposal, there is a possibility that affected parties may not have realized that their interests were at stake in the rulemaking and might not have submitted comments to protect their interests. In light of this potential problem, courts have held that agencies may not make material alterations in the proposal without conducting a second round of notice and comment on the new proposal. The standard has also been stated as the "logical outgrowth" test—final rules must be the logical outgrowth of the original proposal and the comments received. The basic principle is the same—all affected parties must be on notice that their interests are at stake so that they have a reasonable opportunity to submit comments.

3 *See United States v. Nova Scotia Food Prods. Corp.*, 568 F.2d 240 (2d Cir. 1977).

4 No provision of the APA prohibits ex parte communication in informal rulemaking. However, some courts have held that ex parte communications violate §553 because they sidestep the public comment process, create a secret record, and deprive others of an adequate opportunity to comment. While some courts have stated that agencies should refuse to receive ex parte comments, others have been less strict and require only that agencies place all important ex parte comments on the public rulemaking record.

5 *See Association of National Advertisers, Inc. v. FTC*, 627 F.2d 1151 (D.C. Cir. 1979), *cert. denied*, 447 U.S. 921 (1980). The APA does not address prejudgment in rulemaking, and perhaps because of this, courts have never disqualified a decision-maker under this standard. This standard is much less demanding than the standard for prejudgment in adjudication, where the appearance that the decision-maker has in some measure prejudged the facts or law of an adjudicatory dispute can result in disqualification.

6 APA §552(a)(1)(D).

7 APA §553 (c).

8 APA §552(a). *See also Morton v. Ruiz*, 415 U.S. 199 (1974). A party with actual notice of the rule cannot complain that the rule was not published in the *Federal Register*. Thus, where rules affect a small number of parties, the agency may personally serve parties with copies of the rule.

9 *See United States v. Nova Scotia Food Prods. Corp.*

10 Some courts had held that for complicated rules, agencies must employ procedures in addition to those specified in the APA or other applicable statutes or rules. The Supreme Court, in *Vermont Yankee Nuclear Power Corp. v. NRDC*, 435 U.S. 519 (1978), rejected all such holdings and stated emphatically that, absent unconstitutionality, courts have no authority to require agencies to employ procedures other than those required by statute or rule.

FIGURE 8

DUE PROCESS AND ADJUDICATION

Use this chart to determine when due process requires adjudication and, if so, how much process is due before government takes adverse action.

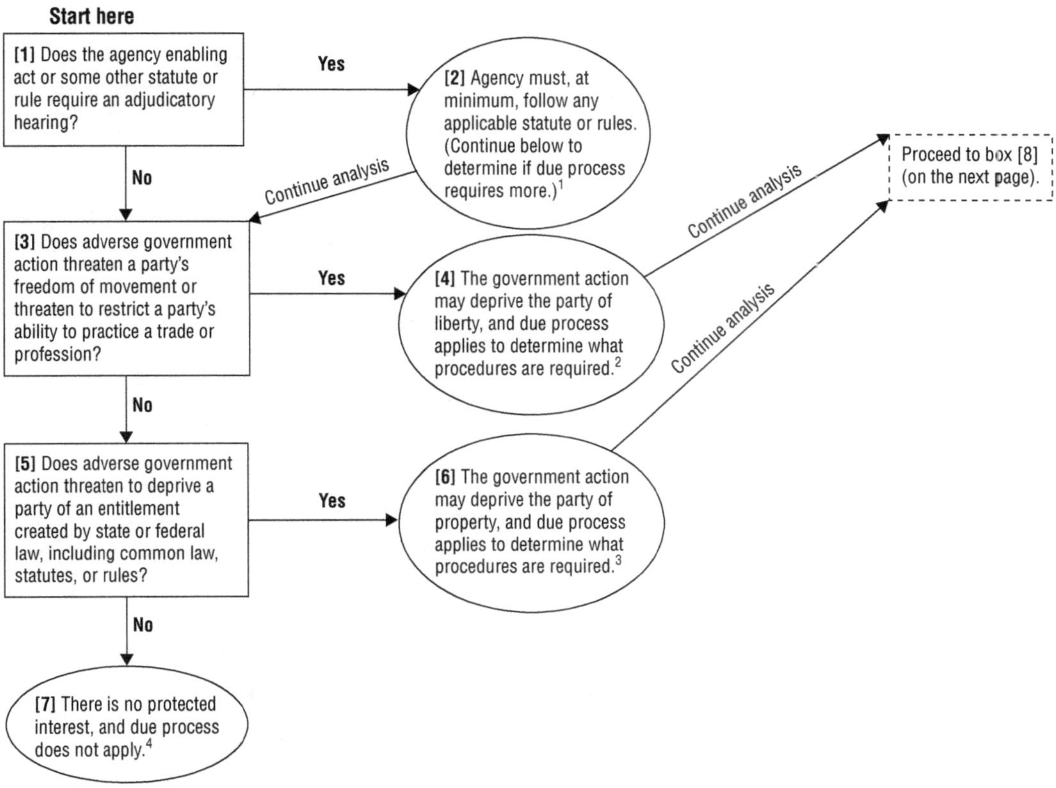

continues on next page

See footnotes after final page of chart

FIGURE 8 (*cont.*)

DUE PROCESS AND ADJUDICATION

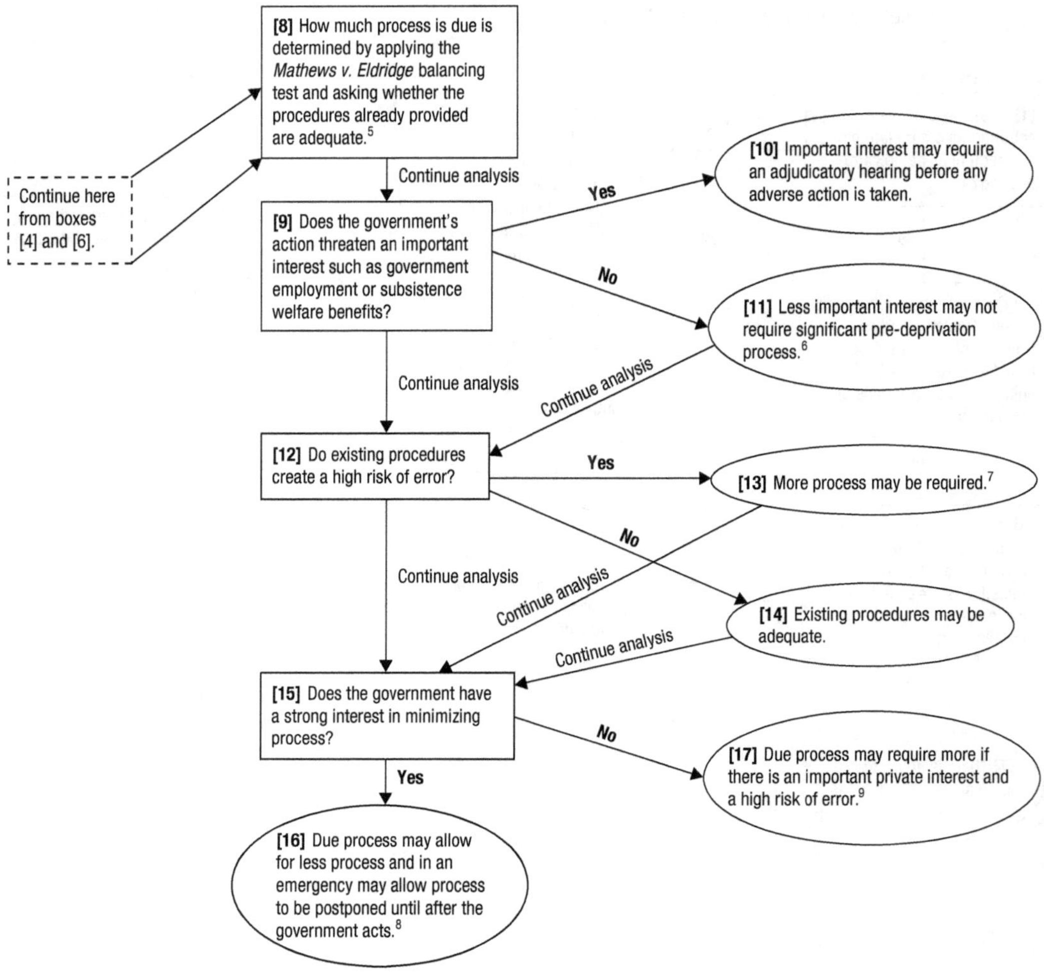

Notes to Figure 8

DUE PROCESS AND ADJUDICATION

1 Agencies must provide whatever process is required by applicable statutes and rules. However, it should be noted that courts, for policy reasons, construe statutes, whenever possible, to maximize agency flexibility and thus do not favor construing statutes to require agencies to conduct formal adjudicatory hearings. It is extremely unlikely in the administrative context that due process will ever require more process than a full adjudicatory hearing under APA §§554, 556, and 557.

2 Liberty interests are created by the Constitution and include such basic rights as the right to freedom from restraint, the right to bodily integrity, and the right to engage in a chosen occupation. Such interests may be restricted by government, but only pursuant to procedures that comport with due process.

3 Property interests are not created by the Constitution but rather are created by an external source of law such as a statute, a rule of common law, or a recognized government practice. The basic test for the existence of property is whether some source of law creates a legitimate claim of entitlement rather than a unilateral expectation. A legitimate claim of entitlement exists when there are legally prescribed criteria for evaluating the propriety of government action, such as a for-cause requirement for termination of government employment. When government action is purely discretionary, such as at-will government employment, there is no entitlement and thus no property interest.

4 Interests in life are not addressed here as they are rarely at issue in administrative law.

5 The *Mathews v. Eldridge* balancing test governs how much process is due when government action threatens to deprive a party of a protected interest. Existing procedures are used as a baseline, and the test is used to determine whether due process requires more. Under that test, the court considers the strength of the regulated party's interest, the likelihood that additional procedure will produce more accurate results, and the government's interest in minimizing process. When the regulated party's interests are relatively weak and existing procedures already produce a high degree of accuracy, due process may not require more than what is already provided. On the other hand, when the regulated party's interests are relatively strong, such as the interest in subsistence welfare payments, and existing procedures produce a high likelihood of error, due process may require relatively formal procedures before government can take even temporary adverse action. The test is not precise, and each factor simply nudges the decision in one direction or another.

6 Claimants often seek a pre-deprivation adjudicatory hearing, while government prefers to postpone the hearing until after it takes action. The Supreme Court has required pre-deprivation hearings when welfare benefits and government employment are at stake, but has not required much in the way of pre-deprivation process in other situations, such as the termination of disability benefits, which are not based on the wealth of the recipient.

7 Typically, courts would add requirements such as an oral hearing, confrontation and cross-examination of adverse witnesses, a closed record (no ex parte contacts or nonrecord evidence), and an impartial decision-maker. Regarding the impartial decision-maker, the decision-maker may not have a significant pecuniary or other interest in the outcome of the case and may not have expressed views indicating prejudgment. Bias and prejudgment raise a substantial likelihood of an erroneous decision.

8 Where it is impractical for government to hold an advance hearing or where an emergency exists, such as contaminated or adulterated food, the Court has allowed virtually all process to be postponed until after the adverse action has already been taken. Also, in *Mathews v. Eldridge* itself, the Court noted that the unlikelihood that the government would be able to recoup disability payments made in error militated in favor of postponing the hearing until after benefits had been suspended.

9 It's not that the lack of a government interest in minimizing process strengthens a claim for more process; it's that, all other things being equal, the lack of such a government interest means that it is more likely that a court would require more process.

FIGURE 9

INFORMATION GATHERING AND INSPECTIONS

Use this chart to analyze whether an agency may gather information or conduct an inspection.

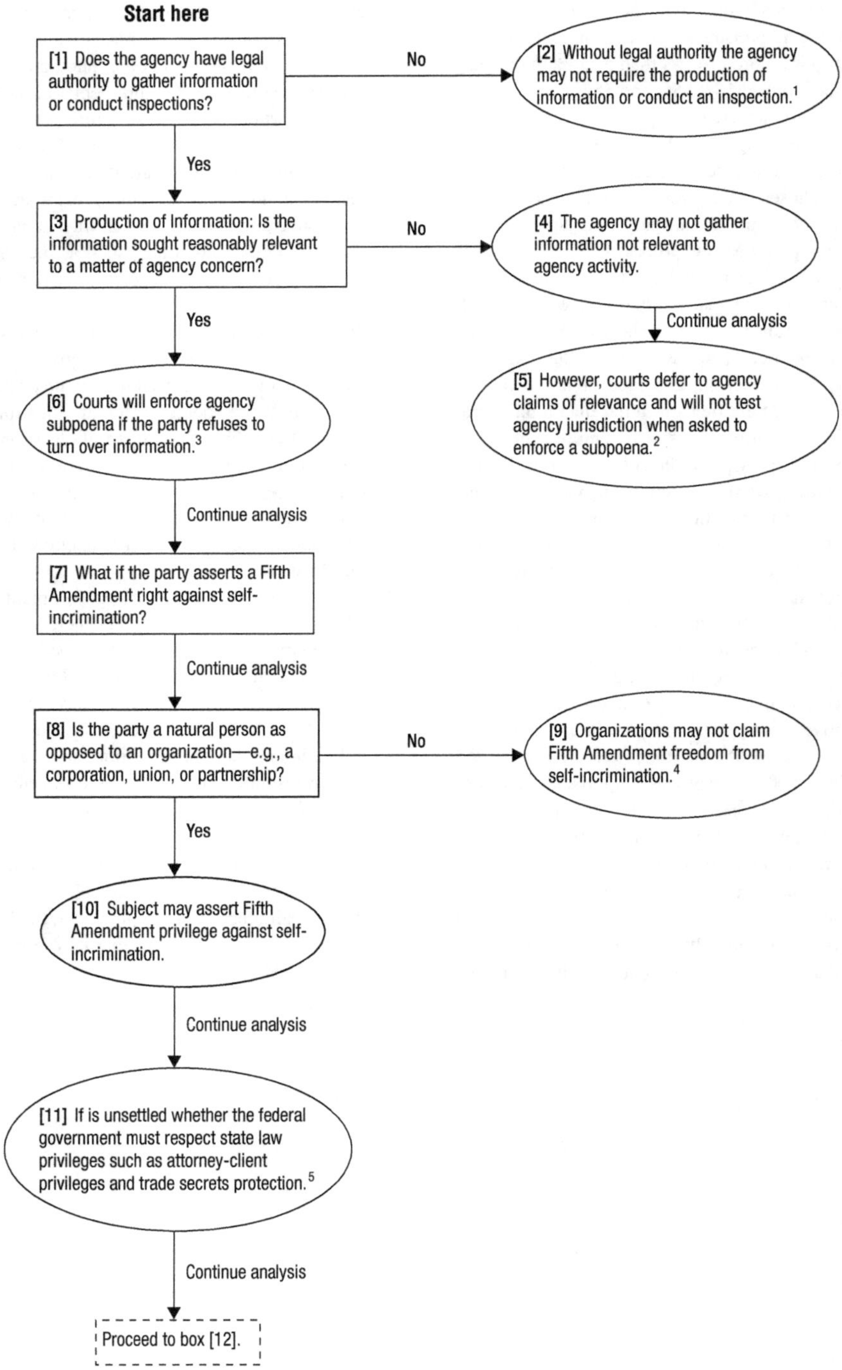

continues on next page

See footnotes after final page of chart

FIGURE 9 (*cont.*)

INFORMATION GATHERING AND INSPECTIONS

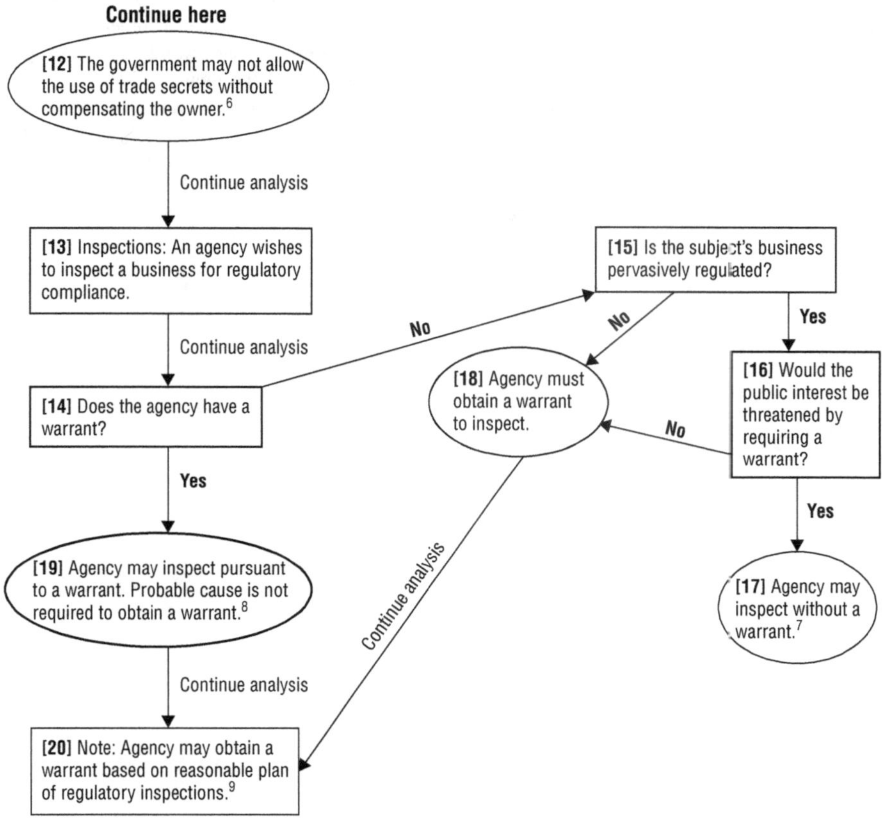

Notes to Figure 9

INFORMATION GATHERING AND INSPECTIONS

1 APA §555(c).

2 *See United States v. Morton Salt Co.*, 338 U.S. 632 (1950).

3 *See United States v. Sturm, Ruger & Co.*, 84 F.3d 1 (1st Cir. 1996).

4 *See Bellis v. United States*, 417 U.S. 85 (1974) (partner in a small law firm has no Fifth Amendment right to withhold partnership records). The Court has held that a natural person who is the custodian of business records may not assert a Fifth Amendment right against turning over business records even if the existence of the records would incriminate the person. *See Braswell v. United States*, 487 U.S. 99 (1988).

5 In *University of Pennsylvania v. EEOC*, 493 U.S. 182 (1990), the court upheld an order to turn over university records even if state law might have recognized a privilege based on academic freedom.

6 *See Ruckelshaus v. Monsanto Co.*, 467 U.S. 986 (1984).

7 *See Donovan v. Dewey*, 452 U.S. 594 (1981); *New York v. Burger*, 482 U.S. 691 (1987).

8 *See Marshall v. Barlow's Inc.*, 436 U.S. 307 (1978).

9 *Id.*

FIGURE 10

FEDERAL TORT CLAIMS

Use this chart to analyze the liability of the federal government and federal officials for tortious conduct.

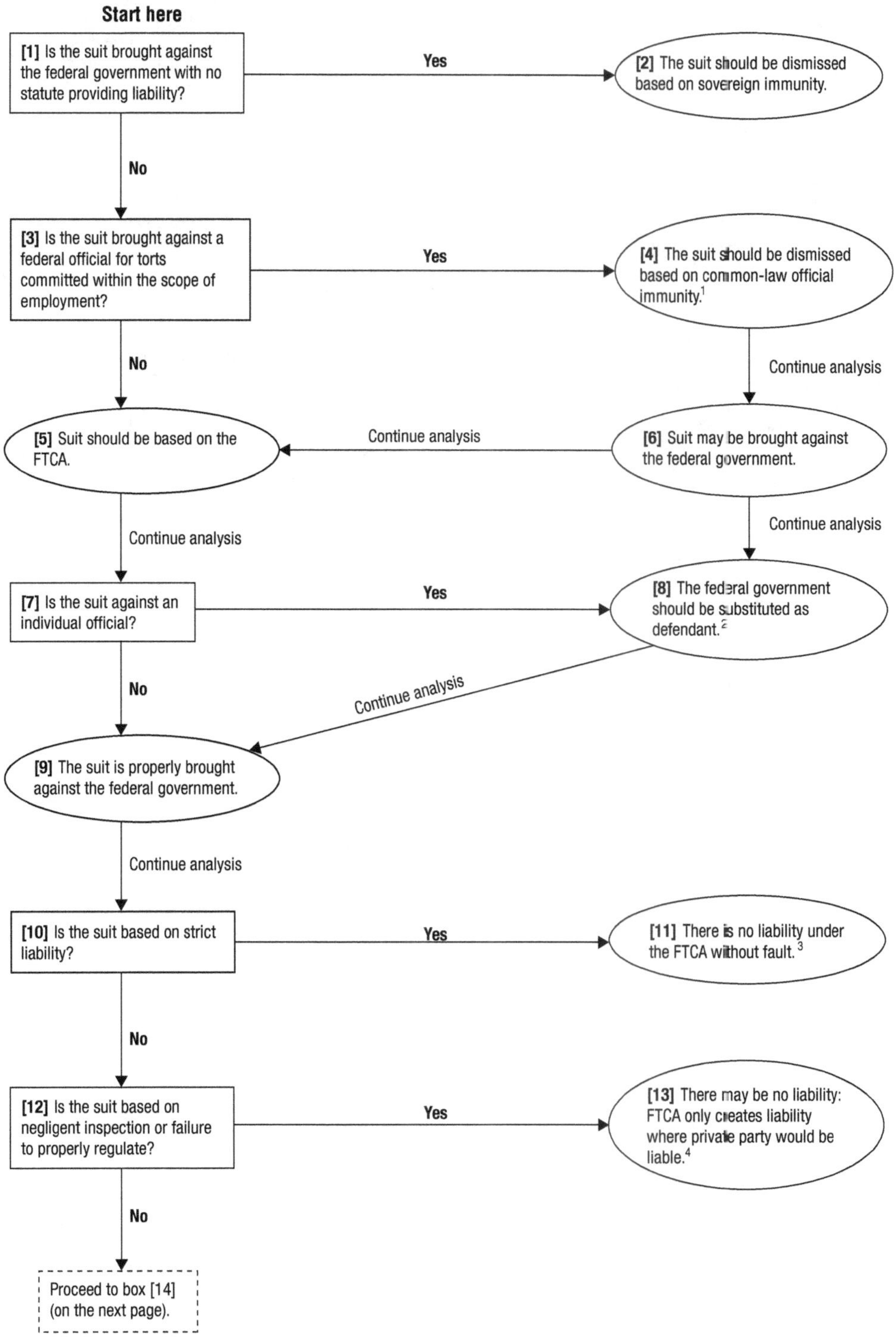

continues on next page

See footnotes after final page of chart

FIGURE 10 (*cont.*)

FEDERAL TORT CLAIMS

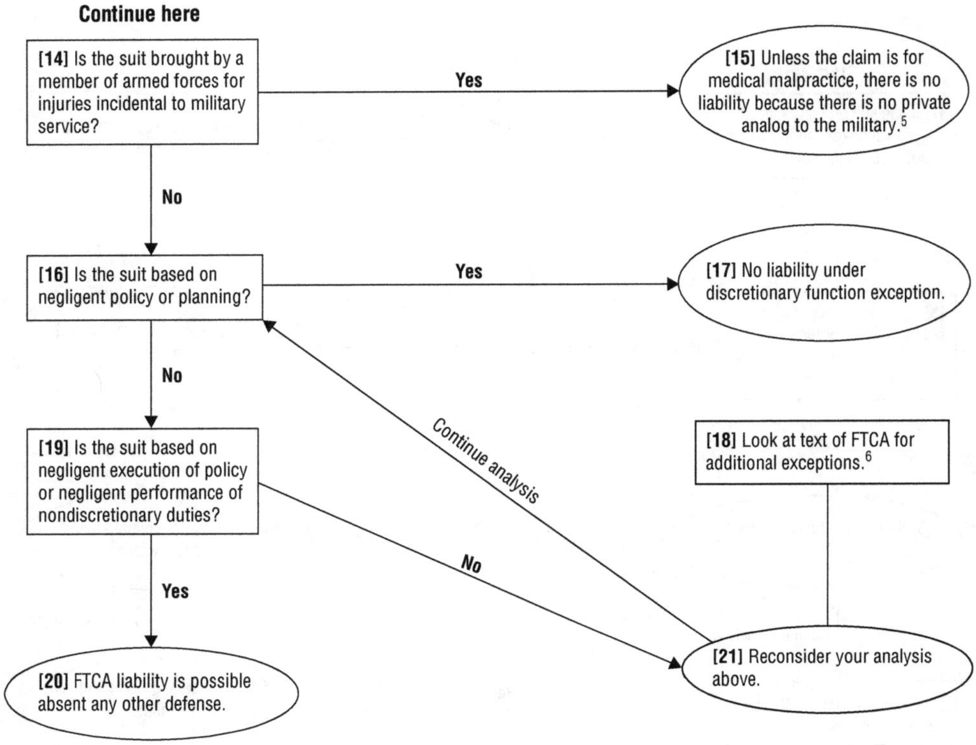

Notes to Figure 10

FEDERAL TORT CLAIMS

[1] *Barr v. Matteo*, 360 U.S. 564 (1959).

[2] Under the Federal Tort Claims Act (FTCA), any tort suit against an individual federal official should be dismissed and the federal government should be substituted as defendant. The official is not liable even if it turns out that the federal government has a good defense in the particular case. The FTCA, in effect, displaces all other tort-based liability against federal officials.

[3] The FTCA creates federal government liability for a "negligent or wrongful act or omission." This language has been interpreted to bar liability without fault, such as strict liability. *See Laird v. Nelms*, 406 U.S. 797 (1972).

[4] The FTCA provides for liability "in the same manner and to the same extent as a private individual under like circumstances." This language has sometimes been interpreted to mean that there is no liability for conduct normally engaged in only by government because there is no analogous private liability. However, the Supreme Court has also stated that there is no government function exception to liability under the FTCA.

[5] The doctrine underlying this is called the Feres doctrine after *Feres* v. United States, 340 U.S. 135 (1940). and goes beyond injuries suffered while engaged in actual military actions such as battle, including, for example, exposure to toxic substances while stationed at a military base in the United States. The doctrine has been criticized because it goes beyond the text of the FTCA which exempts claims arising out of "combatant activities of the military . . . during time of war." In *Feres* itself, the Court barred claims arising out of medical malpractice suffered at the hands of miliary doctors on base. This particular result was overridden by Congress, but the statute doing so left the remainder of the *Feres* doctrine intact.

[6] The FTCA has numerous exceptions from liability, including claims arising out of losses arising out of postal service errors, claims arising out of the administration of taxes, claims arising out of fiscal operations of the Treasury, claims arising in foreign countries, and more. The most important exception is the discretionary-function exception because it covers a broad range of conduct across the entire spectrum of government activity.

FIGURE 11

CONSTITUTIONAL DAMAGES LIABILITY OF FEDERAL OFFICIALS

Use this chart to determine whether an individual federal official may be liable for damages for constitutional violations. Assume the Constitution has been violated and the plaintiff has been injured.

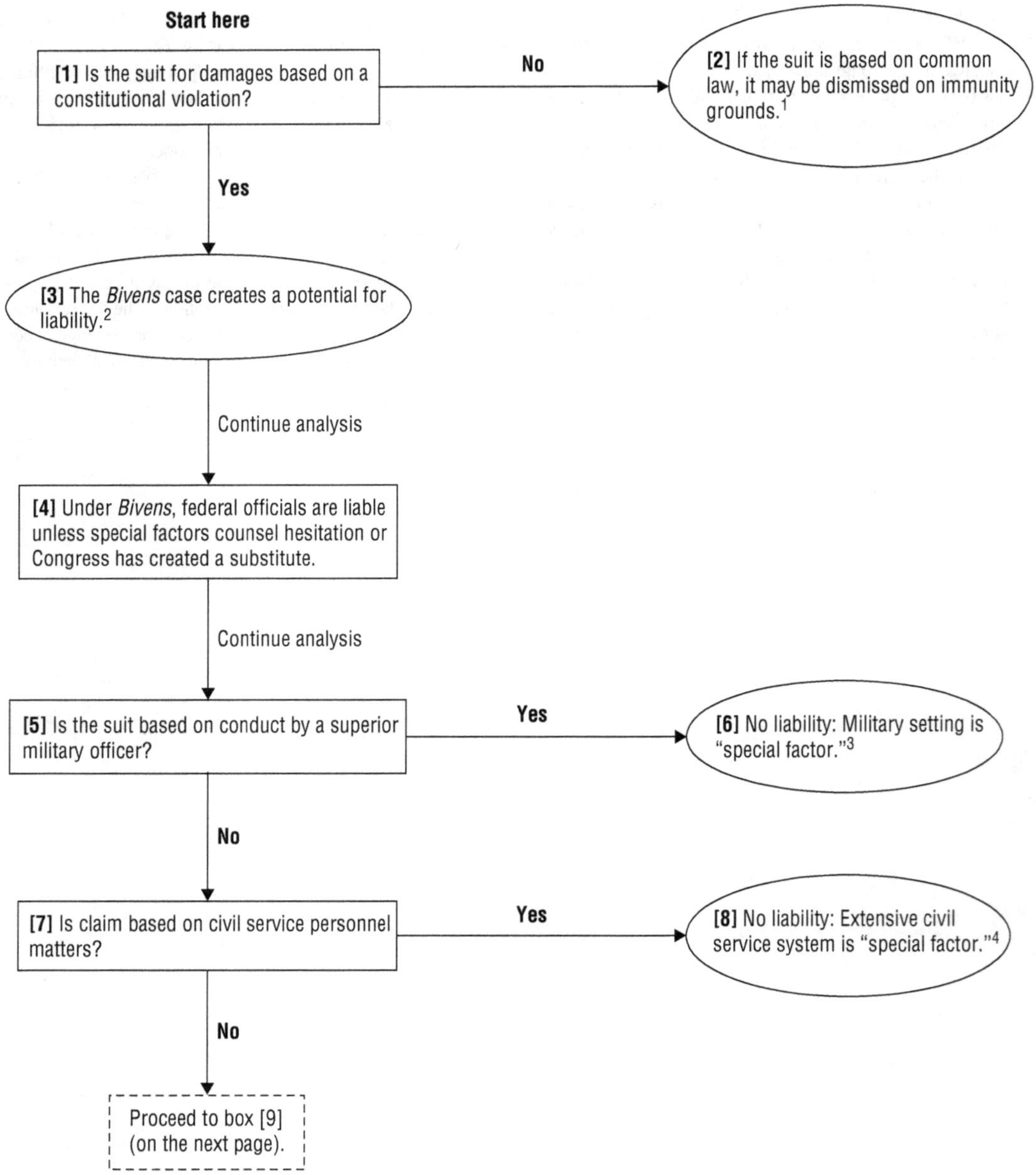

continues on next page

See footnotes after final page of chart

FIGURE 11 (*cont.*)

CONSTITUTIONAL DAMAGES LIABILITY OF FEDERAL OFFICIALS

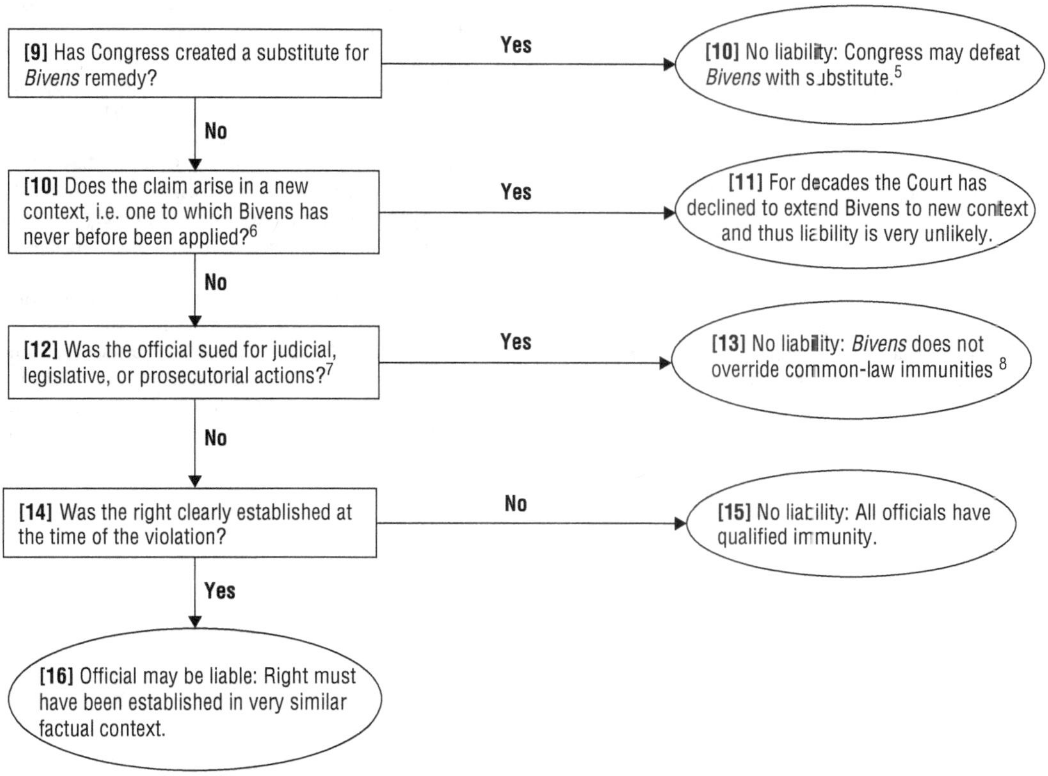

NOTES TO FIGURE 11

CONSTITUTIONAL DAMAGES LIABILITY OF FEDERAL OFFICIALS

1 *Barr v. Matteo*, 360 U.S. 564 (1959), holds that federal officials may assert immunity from suit for damages based on common law. The Federal Tort Claims Act provides that when a federal official is sued for damages based on common law-type claims, the federal government is substituted as defendant and the official is not liable even if the federal government turns out also to be not liable.

2 *Bivens v. Six Unknown Named Agents of Federal Bureau of Narcotics*, 403 U.S. 388 (1971).

3 *Chappell v. Wallace*, 462 U.S. 296 (1983).

4 *Bush v. Lucas*, 762 U.S. 367 (1983).

5 It is not sufficient that a parallel remedy is available. Rather, Congress must designate that the alternative remedy is a substitute for the *Bivens* remedy. *See Carlson v. Green*, 446 U.S. 14 (1980), in which the *Bivens* remedy was allowed to coexist with a remedy against the government under the Federal Tort Claims Act. However, in some cases, the existence of a parallel remedy has contributed to a finding of "special factors counseling hesitation" without a declaration that the *Bivens* remedy has been displaced. *See, e.g., Bush v. Lucas.*

6 E.g. *Wilkie v. Robbins*, 551 U.S. 537 (2007).

7 The *Bivens* action does not override traditional common-law immunities which held that judges, legislators, and prosecutors were absolutely immune from damages liability. The Supreme Court applies a functional approach to determine when an official is shielded by absolute immunity. Administrative officials performing judicial, legislative, and prosecutorial functions are also absolutely immune. However, absolute immunity does not extend to functions other than those for which the immunity exists, For example, a judge is absolutely immune from damages for judicial decisions, but is not absolutely immune from claims arising out of administrative actions such as hiring and firing court personnel.

8 The same immunities apply in cases brought against state and local officials under 42 U.S.C. §1983.

FIGURE 12

FREEDOM OF INFORMATION

Use this chart to analyze issues regarding the requirements of the Freedom of Information Act (FOIA).

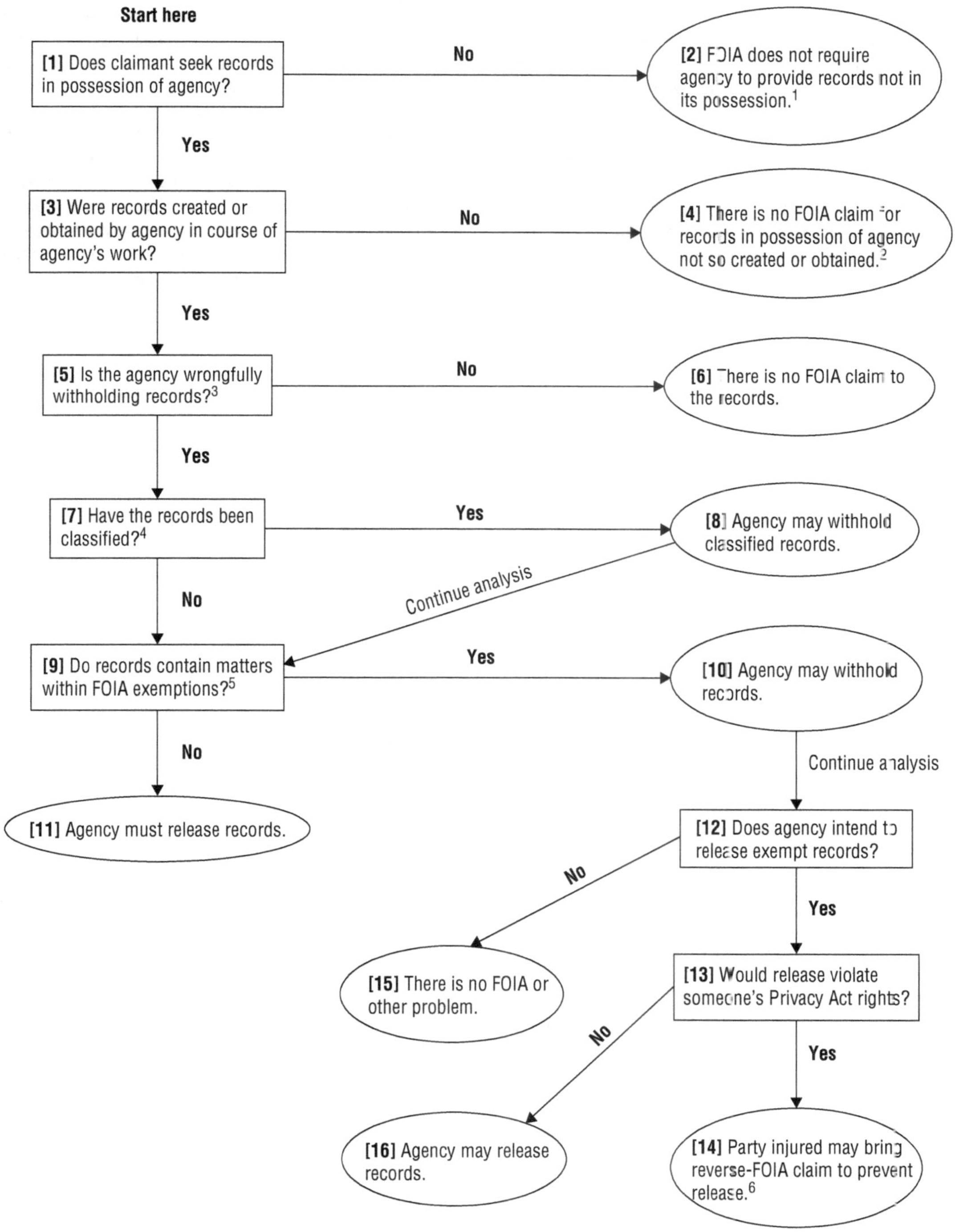

Notes to Figure 12

FREEDOM OF INFORMATION

[1] *Kissinger v. Reporters Committee for Freedom of the Press*, 445 U.S. 136 (1980). FOIA creates liability only when records are "wrongfully withheld." Records are not wrongfully withheld if they are not in the agency's possession.

[2] For example, FOIA does not require an agency to turn over documents that an official keeps in an agency office if the documents were not created or obtained as part of agency activities.

[3] "Wrongfully withholding" means simply that the agency is not providing them when FOIA requires it to. See also footnote 1 to this chart.

[4] FOIA contains an exception for records that have been classified under an executive order "to be kept secret in the interest of national defense or foreign policy." The records must have been actually so classified, not merely classifiable.

[5] FOIA contains a long list of exemptions from disclosure, including personnel matters, trade secrets, records compiled for law enforcement purposes, records regarding regulation of financial institutions, and geological information. If records contain some exempt material along with material that is not exempt, the agency must disclose the nonexempt material if it can be segregated from the exempt material.

[6] The Privacy Act prohibits agencies from disclosing records concerning an individual without that individual's consent. It does not, however, prohibit disclosure of records that would otherwise be subject to disclosure under FOIA. The Court has recognized a claim under FOIA, known as reverse-FOIA, to prevent an agency from disclosing records that are not required by FOIA to be disclosed and would violate an individual's privacy interests.

CAPSULE SUMMARY

CAPSULE SUMMARY

SUMMARY OF CONTENTS

To maximize the usefulness of this Capsule Summary, the focus of discussion reflects the importance of material that is especially helpful for exam preparation. Thus, some levels of the outline that are discussed in the main text are not discussed here, since—while they provide important background material—they are less significant once the reader begins to prepare for the exam.

CHAPTER 1

INTRODUCTION TO STUDYING ADMINISTRATIVE LAW

I. OVERVIEW OF ADMINISTRATIVE LAW

Administrative law regulates the exercise of authority by executive officials including officials of independent agencies.

A. Administrative Law Derives Mainly from Seven Sources

1. The Constitution
2. The Administrative Procedure Act
3. Particular agency-enabling acts
4. Administrative common law
5. Other general statutes
6. Agency rules
7. Presidential directives

B. The Study of Administrative Law: In studying administrative law, the focus is on the source and limits of agency power; potential constitutional limitations on agency power, especially separation of powers; and the procedural requirements placed on the agency by the Constitution, the Administrative Procedure Act (APA), the agency's enabling act, and any other administrative law doctrine.

C. Judicial Review: Judicial review is the mechanism for enforcing procedural and substantive constraints on agency action. Thus, it is vital to be aware of whether judicial review is available, and if so, what standard of judicial review governs.

D. Enforcement: Regulatory norms are enforceable by agencies and sometimes also by private parties affected by alleged violations of regulatory norms. It is important to be aware of the enforcement tools available to both sets of potential enforcers.

II. THE ORIGINS AND ROLES OF ADMINISTRATIVE AGENCIES

The administrative state, as we know it, began in 1887 with the creation of the Interstate Commerce Commission, although the antecedents to the administrative state go back to the beginning of the republic.

A. **Structure of the Administrative State:** While most federal administrative agencies are within a department of the executive branch, Congress has designated some agencies as "independent"—not within any department of the federal government and not under the supervision of the President or any cabinet officer. The independent agency form is controversial as a matter of separation of powers because such agencies are shielded from direct supervision by the President.

B. **The Roles of Administrative Agencies:** Administrative agencies, as the name implies, administer government programs established by Congress.

III. THE FUNCTIONS OF ADMINISTRATIVE AGENCIES

Administrative agencies perform a wide variety of functions in the United States at the local, state, and federal levels. These functions include distribution of government benefits, the granting of licenses and permits, and policymaking in a wide variety of regulated areas. Agencies employ a wide array of policymaking methods including rulemaking, adjudication, and informal policymaking.

IV. PUBLIC INTEREST AND PUBLIC CHOICE UNDERSTANDINGS OF ADMINISTRATIVE LAW

Public interest theory explains administrative policymaking and the structure of administrative agencies based on the traditional notion that agencies act to further the public good and are structured to maximize their ability to further the public good. Public choice theory, by contrast, explains regulation and the structure of agencies as products of the political process in which parties with political power enlist government coercion to achieve goals that they could not achieve in a free market. Public choice theory explains agency structure as maximizing the ability of parties with power to influence government action, rather than as structures created because of views about good policy.

CHAPTER 2

SEPARATION OF POWERS AND DISTRIBUTION OF ADMINISTRATIVE POWER

I. SEPARATION OF POWERS

Separation of powers is fundamental to understanding the Constitution of the United States. The Constitution contains no explicit reference to separation of powers. Rather, the concept is implicit in the three-branch governmental structure the Constitution creates, and it is embodied in numerous constitutional provisions that establish that structure and the procedures under which the branches operate. Separation of powers generally means that each branch of government is confined to exercising those powers within its particular sphere, and government must follow the procedures specified in the Constitution. For more than a century, the structure of what is often called "the administrative state" has been subject to claims that it violates the separation of powers because of the apparent exercise of what appear to be legislative and judicial powers by agencies and the insulation of agency action from presidential control. The Supreme Court has not, as yet, required major changes to the structure of the administrative state based on these concerns.

II. THE NONDELEGATION DOCTRINE

The nondelegation doctrine prohibits Congress from delegating excessive legislative power to the executive branch.

A. **Historical Origins of the Nondelegation Doctrine:** Early cases stated that the Constitution absolutely prohibited the delegation of legislative authority from Congress to the executive branch. Delegations of discretionary authority to the executive branch were permissible as long as Congress made the legislative decisions and the executive branch merely "filled up the details." The discretion exercised by executive officials was not legislative but rather was discretion inherent in execution of the laws.

B. **The Intelligible Principle Test:** In *J.W. Hampton, Jr. & Co. v. United States*, 276 U.S. 394 (1928), the Court stated that a delegation is permissible when Congress "lay[s] down by legislative act an intelligible principle to which the person or body authorized to fix such rates is directed to conform." The "intelligible principle" standard remains the test for determining whether Congress has delegated too much legislative discretion to the executive branch, although several sitting Justices have expressed willingness to tighten up on delegation.

C. **Delegation during the New Deal:** The Supreme Court greeted New Deal legislation with a great deal of skepticism, and in addition to many decisions invalidating state and federal legislation on other grounds, it struck down three federal statutory provisions on two nondelegation grounds. First, the legislation granted broad enforcement powers without specifying when enforcement was required. *See Panama Refining Co. v. Ryan*, 293 U.S. 388 (1935). Second, power was sometimes delegated to private groups, such as trade associations. *See Carter v. Carter Coal Co.*, 298 U.S. 238 (1936). Each of these features was held unconstitutional.

D. **The Return to a Lenient Nondelegation Doctrine:** Beginning in the 1940s and continuing to the present time, the Court has been very lenient in nondelegation cases, requiring only a minimally intelligible principle for a statute to withstand nondelegation attack. Even though the Court continues to evaluate challenges to delegations on the "intelligible principle" standard, the Court always manages to find sufficient legislative guidance to withstand attack, even in very general legislative instructions and goals.

E. ***Benzene* and Nondelegation:** A hint of a revival of the strict nondelegation doctrine was in the *Benzene* case, in which both the plurality and concurring opinions argued that standardless enforcement discretion under the Occupational Safety and Health Act (OSH Act) created nondelegation problems. *See Industrial Union Department, AFL-CIO v. American Petroleum Institute* (the *Benzene Cases*), 448 U.S. 607 (1980). Justice Stevens's plurality opinion relied on the nondelegation doctrine to limit the Occupational Safety and Health Administration's (OSHA's) authority to prescribe occupational health and safety standards to situations in which a substantial health or safety risk has rendered a workplace "unsafe." Justice Rehnquist's *Benzene* concurrence went further, arguing that the statute violated the nondelegation doctrine because it failed to specify when the agency was required to pursue the goal of a virtually risk-free workplace.

Justice Rehnquist's opinion argued that the Court should reinvigorate the nondelegation doctrine because it serves the three related goals of (1) forcing Congress, the representative branch of government, to make important policy choices; (2) increasing the guidance under which agencies act; and (3) facilitating judicial review by requiring more definite statutory standards against which courts can measure administrative decisions.

F. **Attempted Revival of the Nondelegation Doctrine: *Whitman v. American Trucking Associations, Inc.* and *Gundy*:** Since the *Benzene* case, the Court has rejected several delegation challenges. In *American Trucking Associations, Inc. v. U.S. Environmental Protection Agency*, 175 F.3d 1027 (D.C. Cir. 1999), the D.C. Circuit found a violation of the nondelegation doctrine not so much because the statute lacked an intelligible principle but rather because EPA had not adopted an intelligible principle to confine its own discretion. The Supreme Court reversed, reaffirming the intelligible principle test and rejecting the idea that an agency can cure a delegation violation with its own limiting construction. The Court observed that under the D.C. Circuit's analysis, leaving it to the agency to decide on a limiting construction should itself be a nondelegation violation. *See Whitman v. American Trucking Associations, Inc.*, 531 U.S. 457 (2001). The Court, in *Whitman*, virtually disavowed judicial review of the sufficiency of Congress's intelligible principle. However, in *Gundy v. United States*, 588 U.S. 128 (2019), Justice Gorsuch in dissent, joined by Chief Justice Roberts and Justice Thomas, with agreement from Justice Alito on this point, signaled a willingness to discard the intelligible principle standard and replace it with a more stringent standard.

III. CONGRESSIONAL CONTROL OF ADMINISTRATIVE AGENCIES

A. **Congressional Influence:** Members of Congress attempt to influence agencies through formal and informal means. These include numerous informal contacts, influence over appointments to agencies, and, more formally, controlling agency funding, statutorily restricting agency action, and statutorily overruling regulations.

Congress also attempts to increase its influence on agency action by creating independent agencies that are less subject to presidential control.

B. The Legislative Veto and Review of Regulations: Until the Supreme Court held it unconstitutional, the legislative veto was an important device used by Congress to control agency action. Under legislative veto provisions of many enabling acts, Congress could, without presentment to the President, reject agency action (usually regulations). This could be done, depending on the particular provision, by a vote of both houses of Congress, by one house of Congress, or in some cases, even by a single congressional committee. In *Immigration and Naturalization Service v. Chadha*, 462 U.S. 919 (1983), the Supreme Court held a one-house legislative veto unconstitutional on the grounds that the one-house veto violated the bicameralism and presentment requirements of the Constitution. The Court stated that bicameralism and presentment apply to all congressional actions that affect the legal rights and duties of persons outside the legislative branch. Two-house vetoes are also unconstitutional because they violate the requirement that legislation be presented to the President. Two-house rejections of agency rules, with presentment to the President, as provided for in the Congressional Review Act, are constitutional.

C. Congressional Involvement in Appointment and Removal of Executive Officials

1. **Appointments:** The Appointments Clause of the Constitution provides for presidential appointment, with Senate confirmation, of officers of the United States. The clause allows Congress to specify that inferior officers may be appointed by the President alone, by heads of departments, or by the courts of law. In *Buckley v. Valeo*, 424 U.S. 1 (1976), the Court held that officials appointed under a procedure not provided for in the Appointments Clause may not exercise authority under the laws of the United States. Congress, especially the Senate through its advice and consent power, exercises significant political influence over presidential appointments.

2. **Removal:** Officers of the United States may not be subject to removal by congressional action, except by impeachment by the House and conviction by the Senate. Congress often statutorily restricts the removal of administrative officials, and Congress may delegate the removal power to an official under presidential control. For example, in *Morrison v. Olson*, 487 U.S. 654 (1988), the Court upheld the Independent Counsel Act under which a prosecutor appointed to investigate alleged wrongdoing by executive officials could be removed only by the Attorney General, and only for cause. For more on the constitutionality of removal restrictions, see subsection IV.C below.

3. **Members of Congress may not serve as administrative officials:** The Incompatibility Clause, Article I, Section 6, Clause 2 of the Constitution, forbids members of Congress from holding an executive appointment during their term in Congress. In addition to violating the Incompatibility Clause, it would violate separation of powers for members of Congress to serve as administrators.

IV. EXECUTIVE CONTROL OF ADMINISTRATIVE AGENCIES

A. **Inherent Executive Power:** In *Youngstown Sheet & Tube Co. v. Sawyer*, 343 U.S. 579 (1952), the Supreme Court held that President Truman lacked inherent power, without congressional authorization, to order seizure of the nation's steel mills when they were threatened with a strike during the Korean War. In a famous concurring opinion, Justice Jackson argued that the President's power is at its greatest when acting pursuant to express or implied congressional authorization and at its weakest when acting contrary to Congress's will. Jackson argued that when the President acts with neither support nor disapproval from Congress, the President's power to act may be concurrent with Congress's, and the lack of congressional authorization does not necessarily mean that the President is going beyond executive authority.

B. **The Unitary Executive Theory:** The unitary executive theory holds that the Constitution vests all executive power in the President, and thus any attempt by Congress to insulate officials and agencies from complete presidential control is suspect and probably unconstitutional.

C. **Presidential Appointment and Removal of Executive Officials**

1. **Appointment:** The President, with the advice and consent of the Senate, appoints officers of the United States. Officers of the United States "are government officials who exercise significant discretion pursuant to federal law," *Buckley* and "hold a continuing office established by law." *Lucia v. SEC,* 585 U.S. 237, 247 (2018). Congress may specify that inferior officers are appointed by the President alone, by the heads of departments, or by the courts of law.

   a. **Principal officers:** While there is no clear line between principal officers and inferior officers, principal officers are high-level officials in the executive branch, such as department heads and heads of independent agencies. The Court has also suggested that any official with final decision-making authority for the executive branch may be a principal officer.

   b. **Inferior officers:** Inferior officers are lower-level executive officials who are under the supervision of other executive officials beneath the President. *Edmond v. United States*, 520 U.S. 651, 662-663 (1997). In *Morrison v. Olson*, the Court held that an independent counsel investigating wrongdoing by executive branch officials was an inferior officer because of the limited scope and duration of the independent prosecutor's appointment and the Attorney General's removal power.

   c. **Employees:** Employees are low-level officials who are employed by the federal government but exercise no discretion or authority to administer federal law. They are neither principal nor inferior officers, and thus may be appointed pursuant to procedures other than those provided for in the Appointments Clause, such as a civil service-type appointments process.

2. **Recess appointments:** The Constitution allows the President to make temporary appointments to "fill up all Vacancies that may happen during the recess of the Senate" without senatorial advice or consent. U.S. Const., Art. II, §2, cl. 3. This power may not be used when the Senate claims to be in session while conducting pro forma sessions and, presumptively, during an intrasession break shorter than ten days. *NLRB v. Noel Canning*, 573 U.S. 513 (2014).

3. **Removal:** The Constitution does not mention the removal of officials except through impeachment and conviction. In the absence of statutory restrictions, the President has the power to remove executive officials at will. Congress may, under some circumstances, restrict the President's power to remove executive officials, but Congress itself may not retain advice and consent power over removal of officials or participate in the removal of officials except through impeachment. The current rule is that Congress may restrict removal of heads of multimember independent agencies and inferior officers without policymaking or administrative responsibilities. Further, the Supreme Court has held that Congress may not provide for two levels of for-cause restriction on the removal of an official. In other words, if the heads of an agency are not removable at will, their subordinates must be removable without restriction.

D. Direct Presidential Supervision of Administrative Agencies: The degree to which the President has inherent authority to supervise administrative agencies is an unsettled and controversial area of law. Presidents may use Executive Orders to supervise the actions of executive branch officials, but Presidents may not contravene the law in such orders.

E. The Line Item Veto: The Line Item Veto Act is unconstitutional since it in effect grants the President unilateral power to amend or repeal legislation. *See Clinton v. City of New York*, 524 U.S. 417 (1998). The Act gave the President the power to cancel items in bills after signing the bills. The problem with this is that once the President signed the bill passed by Congress, the entire bill became law, and only further legislation by both houses of Congress could amend or repeal it.

V. ADJUDICATION WITHIN ADMINISTRATIVE AGENCIES

Agency adjudication raises a separation of powers problem because Article III vests the judicial power of the United States in the Article III courts, and it has been argued that administrative agencies usurp that power when they adjudicate cases. However, the Supreme Court has approved of a great deal of agency adjudication as long as administrative agencies adjudicate cases involving public rights or in areas closely connected to federal regulatory programs and do not seize the central attributes of judicial power. Limited jurisdiction, limited powers, the consent of the parties, the availability of Article III jurisdiction, and judicial review and enforcement of judgments in Article III courts are factors that support the constitutionality of administrative adjudication. However, when an agency seeks monetary penalties in actions that resemble common-law claims such as fraud, the subject of the enforcement action is entitled to a trial by jury, which means that the enforcement action must be brought in federal court.

CHAPTER 3

THE AVAILABILITY OF JUDICIAL REVIEW OF ADMINISTRATIVE DECISIONS

I. JURISDICTION

The petition for judicial review must be brought in a court that has jurisdiction over the claim, normally either the district court or court of appeals. In most cases, the choice between the court of appeals and the district court is simple because the agency's governing statute identifies the proper forum for judicial review. Most of these statutes provide for review of administrative action in the court of appeals. If no statute states otherwise, review must be sought in the district court under that court's federal question original jurisdiction. For reasons of judicial economy, courts interpret specific statutes, whenever possible, to direct review to the court of appeals—even in cases of informal agency action where there is no formal agency record.

II. REVIEWABILITY

A. **Presumption in Favor of Judicial Review:** There is a long-standing presumption that judicial review of agency action is available. The Administrative Procedure Act (APA) provisions granting judicial review in favor of persons adversely affected or aggrieved by final agency action reinforce this presumption, subject to APA created exceptions.

B. **Exceptions to Reviewability:** APA §701 specifies two situations in which APA judicial review is not available: when "statutes preclude judicial review," §701(a)(1), and when "agency action is committed to agency discretion by law." §701(a)(2).

1. **Agency action:** Review under the APA is available only for "agency action." The President is not an agency within the meaning of the APA. Further, the Supreme Court has required that the petitioner identify a particular agency action that is being challenged, such as the issuance of a rule or order, or the refusal to do so, holding that APA review is not available to challenge the general manner in which an agency regulates. *See Norton v. Southern Utah Wilderness Alliance*, 542 U.S. 55 (2004).

2. **Statutory preclusion:** For a statute to preclude judicial review, it should explicitly mention judicial review and either preclude it completely or provide for a particular form of judicial review and preclude all others.

3. **"Committed to agency discretion by law":** The traditional understanding of "committed to agency discretion by law" is that judicial review is not available when the governing statutes are drawn in such broad terms that in a given case there is no law to apply. Review may also be "committed to agency discretion by law" when the statute suggests that Congress intended for the agency to have final authority over a decision, or when the agency action is in a category of

administrative decisions that have traditionally been held to be committed to agency discretion.

4. **Reviewability of enforcement discretion:** The Supreme Court has created, under APA §701(a)(2), a strong presumption that agency prosecutorial decisions, such as choosing targets for administrative enforcement, are unreviewable as "committed to agency discretion by law." The presumption exists because few enabling acts contain precise instructions about when an agency must act, and because the decision of when to act and against whom often involves balancing multiple factors such as available resources and effective enforcement policy. The presumption against review of enforcement discretion may be rebutted if the agency's enabling act requires the agency to act under certain specified circumstances or within a certain time period.

5. Despite arguments that it was analogous to enforcement discretion, the Supreme Court has held that decisions not to engage in rulemaking are reviewable, but on a highly deferential standard of review. *Massachusetts v. EPA*, 549 U.S. 497, 527-528 (2007).

C. **Preclusion of Review of Constitutional Questions:** Because precluding judicial review of constitutional challenges raises a serious constitutional question, courts have interpreted statutes precluding judicial review to preclude review only of nonconstitutional questions, while preserving review of constitutional issues. It is unsettled whether and to what degree Congress may bar review of constitutional questions. Further, a statute that precludes judicial review of agency action does not preclude a constitutional challenge to the statute itself, since in such a case the Court reviews a decision by Congress, not the agency. *See Johnson v. Robison*, 415 U.S. 361 (1974).

III. STANDING TO SECURE JUDICIAL REVIEW

A party seeking judicial review must have standing. Constitutional standing doctrine requires that the plaintiff must be injured by the challenged conduct and must stand to gain from a favorable ruling (redressability). In addition to the constitutional injury and redressability requirements, the federal courts have imposed prudential standing limitations that bar plaintiffs from asserting the rights of third parties and from seeking redress for generalized grievances, which affect society as a whole.

There are exceptions to the prudential limitations such as the doctrine that allows third parties to assert the constitutional rights of those who are unable to assert their own rights. The party asserting the rights must still meet the constitutional injury and redressability requirements. Further, because the prudential limitations on standing are judge made and not constitutionally compelled, Congress has the power to overrule them.

A. **Standing: The Old "Legal Right" Test:** Early administrative law standing cases allowed review only on behalf of parties whose own legal rights had been allegedly violated by agency action. Parties injured by agency treatment of others, for example, when an agency loosens regulation on a competitor, lacked standing to seek judicial review of the agency's treatment of the third party or parties.

B. Standing: The "Injury-in-Fact Fairly Traceable" Test: In reaction to criticism of the legal right test, the Court replaced it with the requirement that the plaintiff have suffered an injury-in-fact that is fairly traceable to the challenged conduct and is redressable by a favorable judgment. Further, the plaintiff must be in the zone of interests of the statute under which relief is sought.

1. **Abstract injury not sufficient:** Persons or groups with an abstract interest in a regulatory scheme, such as animal lovers concerned about preserving endangered species, do not have standing without an actual injury. For example, an environmental group does not have standing to challenge the treatment of a wilderness area unless members of the group actually use the area in question, and voters do not have standing to challenge gerrymandering unless they live in an allegedly gerrymandered district.

2. **The injury must be "fairly traceable" to the challenged conduct:** The injury must be "fairly traceable" to the challenged conduct, or in other words, the conduct challenged must have actually caused the injury. While the concept of causation is not particularly difficult to understand, it is often not clear why the Supreme Court finds causation present in some cases and absent in others.

3. **Redressability:** To have standing, the plaintiff must show that the remedy sought will redress the injury. A plaintiff seeking relief against past harm may lack standing on redressability grounds if the harm is not continuing, and the plaintiff is not entitled to damages or any other form of compensation for the past harm.

4. **Procedural injury:** Although a party may challenge an agency action for failure to follow proper procedures, to have standing to do so the plaintiff must have suffered an injury in addition to the denial of alleged procedural rights. The party does not have to show that if proper procedures had been followed, the result of the proceeding would have been different.

C. APA Standing and the Zone of Interests Test: The Supreme Court has held that to have standing in a case brought under the APA, the plaintiff must establish that "the interest sought to be protected by the complainant is arguably within the zone of interests to be protected or regulated by the statute or constitutional guarantee in question." The zone of interests test applies to cases in which the plaintiff seeks to challenge agency treatment of someone else (such as a competitor) and asks whether the plaintiff's interests were considered by or relevant to Congress or the regulatory body in the decision to regulate the third party. Citizens suit provisions usually override prudential limitations on standing and place all persons identified as potential plaintiffs within the zone of interests.

D. Associational Standing: Associations (such as interest groups and trade associations) have standing to litigate their own claims and also the claims of their members as long as the members themselves would have standing to sue, the interests the association is suing over are within the association's purpose, and the litigation will not be adversely affected by the absence of individual plaintiffs.

IV. THE TIMING OF JUDICIAL REVIEW: RIPENESS, FINALITY EXHAUSTION, AND MOOTNESS

Judicial review may not be sought too early (ripeness and finality), too late (mootness), and in some cases, without exhausting administrative remedies.

A. **Ripeness and the APA's Grant of Review of "Final Agency Action":** APA §704's grants of judicial review of "final agency action for which there is no other adequate remedy in a court" is essentially a ripeness requirement, which excludes from review agency action that is not yet complete. Agency action is final when the agency's decision-making process has been completed and the decision has legal consequences. Even though a rule is "final" upon promulgation, the Supreme Court has held that a rule is ripe for review upon promulgation (before enforcement) only if the issues are fit for judicial review and the party seeking review would suffer substantial hardship if review were delayed until after enforcement. *Abbott Laboratories v. Gardner*, 387 U.S. 136, 148 (1967).

B. **Ripeness of Informal Agency Action:** When informal agency action has the effect of granting or denying permission to take a requested course of action, a court might consider it final agency action even though the decision was made without any formal procedures.

C. **Ripeness of Agency Inaction or Refusal to Act:** If the agency formally declines to take action, that decision can be a "final agency action" subject to judicial review. If an agency fails to answer a request to act, the failure to act is ripe for review only in the rare circumstance that agency inaction is the equivalent of a decision not to act or appears from the circumstances to amount to a decision not to act. If an agency is statutorily required to act in an emergency, agency inaction in response to a petition alleging an emergency may amount to a decision that no emergency exists that requires agency action.

D. **Exhaustion of Administrative Remedies Prior to Seeking Judicial Review:** One of the oldest, most established doctrines in administrative law is that challengers must exhaust remedies within the agency before seeking judicial review.

   1. **Exceptions to the exhaustion requirement:** A party is not required to exhaust administrative remedies when (1) exhaustion would cause undue prejudice to the protection of the rights at issue, (2) the administrative agency lacks power to grant effective relief, or (3) the exhaustion would be futile because the administrative body is biased or has predetermined the matter.

   2. **APA exhaustion doctrine:** The Supreme Court has held that if agency action is final under §704, no further exhaustion is required and review is available immediately. Under §704, exhaustion is required only of those remedies expressly required by statute or agency rule and only if agency action is inoperative while internal remedies are exhausted.

E. **Mootness:** A case is moot if there is no longer a live controversy between the parties. For example, if a party is no longer subject to an agency rule or if the agency repeals the rule, a claim for judicial review of the rule may be moot. There are exceptions to mootness: a claim may be heard despite mootness if the claim is "capable of repetition yet evading review" or when the defendant voluntarily ceases the challenged conduct but remains free to resume it.

CHAPTER 4

JUDICIAL REVIEW OF ADMINISTRATIVE ACTION

I. STANDARDS OF JUDICIAL REVIEW UNDER THE APA

APA standards of judicial review govern unless the agency's enabling act contains a provision establishing a standard of review that differs from the applicable APA standard.

A. **APA §706 and Standards of Review:** APA §706 contains the standards of judicial review that apply to agency action.

APA §706(2)(D) applies the substantial evidence test to formal adjudication and formal rulemaking.

APA §706(2)(E) applies de novo review when (1) "the [agency] action is adjudicatory in nature and the agency factfinding procedures are inadequate" or (2) "issues that were not before the agency are raised in a proceeding to enforce nonadjudicatory agency action."

APA §706(2)(A) provides that any agency action should be set aside if it is "arbitrary, capricious, an abuse of discretion, or otherwise not in accordance with law." The arbitrary and capricious test contains no limitation on its applicability, and thus it applies to all reviewable administrative actions. Because it is the most deferential standard of review, parties challenging administrative action prefer de novo or substantial evidence review.

B. **The Record on Review:** APA §706 requires reviewing courts to examine the "whole record." The record consists of the material the agency had before it when it made its decision—not support created after the agency made its decision. The reviewing court looks at the whole record, not just the evidence supporting the agency's decision.

II. THE SUBSTANTIAL EVIDENCE TEST

The substantial evidence test, which governs review of formal agency adjudication and formal rulemaking, is the same standard that governs whether a judge should submit an issue to a jury rather than direct a verdict. That standard is whether such relevant evidence exists as a reasonable mind might accept as adequate to support a conclusion. The "whole record" requirement means that a decision might fail the substantial evidence test even though it is supported by some evidence, when that evidence is overwhelmed by evidence to the contrary.

A. **Witness Credibility:** When an agency's decision is based, in whole or in part, on the credibility of the witnesses, the agency's decision is entitled to great deference because the reviewing court reviews only the paper record, without the opportunity to observe the demeanor of the witnesses.

B. **Agency Reversals of ALJ Decisions:** When an agency reverses the decision of the trier of fact on appeal within the agency, the initial decision is part of the "whole record," and the reviewing court must take the reversal into account in deciding whether the agency's decision is supported by substantial evidence.

III. DE NOVO REVIEW OF QUESTIONS OF FACT

Where agency adjudicatory fact-finding procedures are inadequate or when new factual issues arise in an action to enforce nonadjudicatory agency action, the regulated party might be entitled to de novo review of the facts. De novo review means that the facts are retried in the court, and no deference is paid to agency factual conclusions.

IV. REVIEW OF QUESTIONS OF LAW

There are competing traditions regarding judicial review of agency conclusions of law—one under which courts review questions of law de novo and another under which courts defer to agency interpretations of the statutes they administer. Courts have traditionally shown the greatest deference to agency decisions involving the applications of law to particular facts. Although the Court no longer distinguishes between issues of statutory authority to regulate and other statutory issues, traditionally courts have decided issues of agency statutory authority without deferring to the agency's interpretation of its enabling act.

A. ***Chevron:*** In *Chevron, U.S.A., Inc. v. Natural Resources Defense Council, Inc.*, 467 U.S. 837 (1984), the Court stated that unless Congress has directly spoken to the precise issue in question, courts should defer to agencies on pure questions of statutory interpretation as long as the agency arrived at a reasonable or permissible construction of the statute. Recently, the Court overruled Chevron and embraced de novo review of questions of law, although it suggested that agency constructions may be persuasive in some circumstances.

B. **Alternative Versions of *Chevron* Step One: *Cardoza-Fonseca*, Plain Meaning, and Extraordinary Cases:** The Court sometimes stated that under *Chevron*, the reviewing court should attempt to ascertain Congress's intent using "traditional tools of statutory construction." These include the language, structure, purpose, and legislative history of the statute being construed, and other interpretive devices such as the canons of statutory interpretation. *See INS v. Cardoza-Fonseca*, 480 U.S. 421, 447 (1987). In some cases, the Court's analysis centered on one of the "traditional tools"—namely, the plain meaning rule. In still other cases, the Court denominated the case "extraordinary" because the issues are important or have great economic consequences and found congressional intent without following the *Chevron* analysis.

C. ***Chevron* Step Two:** Permissible or Reasonable Construction: If a statute is ambiguous, or if Congress has left a gap for the agency to fill, an agency's interpretation was permissible under *Chevron* if it is "a sufficiently rational one to preclude a court from substituting its judgment for that of the [agency]." *Young v. Community Nutrition Institute*, 476 U.S. 974, 981 (1986). This is very deferential.

D. **When *Chevron* Applied:** *Chevron* applied to agency interpretation of a statute administered by the agency, rendered in relatively formal settings such as rulemaking and adjudication. Under *United States v. Mead Corp.*, 533 U.S. 218 (2001), it does not apply to agency statutory interpretations rendered less formally, such as in a ruling letter. In such cases, *Skidmore* deference may apply. Under *Skidmore*, courts defer to agency statutory interpretations on a sliding scale based on the formality of the process, the importance of agency expertise, and the degree to which the agency's reasoning is persuasive.

E. **Loper Bright:** In *Loper Bright Enterprises v. Raimondo*, 144 S. Ct. 2244 (2024), the Supreme Court overruled *Chevron*. It found *Chevron* was inconsistent with the APA's instruction that "the reviewing court shall decide all relevant questions of law, interpret constitutional and statutory provisions, and determine the meaning or applicability of the terms of an agency action." However, the Court endorsed *Skidmore*'s observation that courts might resort to agency views of statutory meaning for guidance, especially regarding interpretations issued contemporaneously with the statute at issue, implicate agency expertise, and which have remained consistent over time. *Skidmore v. Swift & Co.*, 323 U.S. 134 (1944).

F. **The Major Questions Doctrine (MQD)**: In a series of relatively recent decisions, the Supreme Court has articulated and elaborated on the MQD which, in a nutshell, holds that unless clearly delegated by Congress, agencies lack the power to take highly consequential actions in areas of great economic and political significance. Cases include the imposition of an eviction moratorium during the COVID-19 pandemic, the requirement that all employees in large businesses be vaccinated against the virus (or test weekly and wear masks at work) and the EPA's clean power plan which would have compelled power companies to stop burning coal. This means that more than the general language typical of regulatory statutes is needed before the Court will an agency's assertion of authority to act in an area it deems to present a "major question."

G. **Agency Interpretations of Agency Regulations:** Courts defer to agency interpretations of their own regulations under *Bowles v. Seminole Rock & Sand Co.*, 325 U.S. 410 (1945) and *Auer v. Robbins*, 519 U.S. 452 (1997). Under *Auer* deference, a court defers to an agency's interpretation of its own regulations "unless it is plainly erroneous or inconsistent with the regulation." 325 U.S. at 414. *Auer* does not apply unless the court concludes that, after applying the traditional tools of construction, the regulation is "genuinely ambiguous," that the construction is the agency's authoritative position, that the construction implicates agency expertise, and that the agency's construction reflects "fair and considered judgment" not a "convenient litigating position" or a post hoc rationalization. *Auer* deference may not survive *Loper-Bright*'s overruling of *Chevron* since it also seems inconsistent with the APA.

V. REVIEW OF QUESTIONS OF POLICY

A. Informal Rulemaking and Informal Agency Action: Courts review most agency policy decisions under the arbitrary and capricious test, which applies to informal rulemaking and informal agency action. The arbitrary and capricious test requires that agencies make decisions:

1. "based on a consideration of the relevant factors," including alternatives to the agency's proposal;
2. without "a clear error of judgment"; and
3. under the correct legal standard.

The Court has also stated that:

4. while the arbitrary and capricious inquiry is "searching and careful,"
5. the standard of review is "a narrow one [and t]he court is not empowered to substitute its judgment for that of the agency."

Citizens to Preserve Overton Park v. Volpe, 401 U.S. 402, 416-417 (1971).

The relevant factors are those factors mentioned in governing statutes. As proof that they considered all relevant factors, courts require agencies to explain their decisions on major issues raised during the decision-making process. Agencies may not consider factors not identified in the agency's governing statute.

Agency policy changes are also reviewed under the deferential arbitrary, capricious standard. However, the agency must demonstrate that it is aware that it is making the change and it must explain the change.

B. The Special Case of the Standard of Review of Deregulation: Deregulation is normally reviewed under the same test that applies to the initial promulgation of the regulation being relaxed or rescinded. In most cases of informal rulemaking, this means the arbitrary and capricious test. The Court has rejected arguments that deregulation decisions should be reviewed under the same standard that governs a refusal to regulate in the first place.

VI. REMEDIES ON JUDICIAL REVIEW

Reviewing courts have the power under APA §706 to "hold unlawful and set aside" agency action found not to meet the applicable standard of review. However, courts often remand matters to the agency for further consideration without ordering the agency to change its decision. This gives agencies the opportunity to cure any defects identified on judicial review. In recent years, federal courts have increasingly issued nationwide injunctions against what they find to be unlawful agency action, which has been controversial in part because the practice encourages parties to seek out a sympathetic district judge.

CHAPTER 5

AGENCY CHOICE OF PROCEDURAL MODE

I. DUE PROCESS CONSTRAINTS ON CHOICE OF PROCEDURE

In most cases the choice between rulemaking and adjudication is left to Congress or to the agency under delegation from Congress. When an agency makes a decision applicable generally to an entire class of parties, a legislative procedure is sufficient to satisfy due process. *See Bi-Metallic Investment Co. v. State Board of Equalization*, 239 U.S. 441 (1915). However, under *Londoner v. Denver*, 210 U.S. 373 (1908), due process requires an adjudicatory hearing when the agency's decision is particularized to the situation of a regulated party.

II. STATUTORY CONSTRAINTS AND AGENCY CHOICE OF POLICYMAKING PROCEDURE

The APA divides all agency action into two models—rulemaking and adjudication—but says very little about when each is required except that agencies must use rulemaking to promulgate a rule, and they must employ an adjudicatory process to issue orders against regulated parties. Agencies make rule-like determinations in both rulemaking and adjudication, and either is proper as long as the agency has the power to use the particular procedure and all procedural requirements are observed. In the absence of clear statutory constraints, agency choice of policymaking mode is in the discretion of the agency. *SEC v. Chenery Corp.*, 332 U.S. 194 (1947). Rulemaking is the procedure agencies must use to issue actual rules, i.e., rules placed in the Code of Federal Regulations.

A. **Agency Discretion to Make Policy by Rule:** Rulemaking is the preferred policymaking method for agencies because it allows agencies to make clear, comprehensive decisions in a legislative process in which the agency can benefit from extensive public input and thus make better policy decisions. Rulemaking is also fair because it establishes rules that govern all regulated parties at once rather than singling out parties at different times, which may occur when an agency brings an enforcement action against one regulated party at a time. Agencies often make rules in rulemaking and then apply those rules in subsequent adjudicatory proceedings.

B. **Rulemaking and the Right to a Hearing:** Agencies often use rulemaking to determine whether particular conduct violates a regulatory statute. Regulated parties have argued that when Congress establishes a hearing process to determine regulatory violations, the rulemaking violates their right to a hearing on all issues. This argument has been rejected, with a caveat that the agency must provide an opportunity for the party to argue that the rule should not apply in the particular case. *United States v. Storer Broadcasting Co.*, 351 U.S. 192 (1956).

C. **Agency Power to Make Policy by Adjudication:** Agencies often announce new rules of decision in an opinion arising from an adjudication. This practice has been challenged on the ground that the APA's definitions require rulemaking as the procedure for formulating general rules, especially when the agency announces in an adjudication a new rule of decision that will be applied prospectively only. The Supreme Court has rejected these challenges, although not definitively, stating that the choice between adjudication and rulemaking lies largely within the discretion of the agency.

III. INFORMAL POLICYMAKING

A. **Exemptions from §553:** APA §553 exempts from all of its requirements rules that are in the areas of the military, foreign affairs, agency management, personnel, public property, loans, grants, benefits, and contracts. Section 553 also exempts, from its notice-and-comment requirements, nonlegislative rules such as interpretive rules, general statements of policy, and rules of agency organization or practice. Further, §553(b) allows agencies to dispense with notice-and-comment procedures when it finds that such procedures are "impracticable, unnecessary or contrary to the public interest."

1. **Nonlegislative rule:** A nonlegislative rule is a rule that has no legal effect. Rather, it interprets existing legal obligations (interpretive rule) or states the agency's view on a matter of policy without creating legal rights or obligations (general statement of policy). Nonlegislative rules must be published in the Federal Register. Agencies may not give legal effect to nonlegislative rules.

B. **Policymaking by Manual or Other Internal Document:** When an agency makes policy without going through either rulemaking or adjudication, the APA requires that any rule be published in the Federal Register, or it may not be used against any party not having actual notice of it. APA §552(a)(1). *See Morton v. Ruiz*, 415 U.S. 199 (1974).

C. **Agencies' Obligation to Follow Their Own Procedural Rules:** Agencies must follow any procedural rules they have formally adopted through notice-and-comment procedures, but informally adopted rules may be ignored unless a party that the agency intended to benefit detrimentally relied on the informally adopted procedural rule. *See American Farm Lines v. Black Ball Freight Service*, 397 U.S. 532 (1970); *Schweiker v. Hansen*, 450 U.S. 785 (1981).

D. **Informal Policymaking Generally: When May an Agency Act without Adjudication or Rulemaking?** Agencies often decide policy matters in the course of granting or denying applications or petitions informally (without using either an adjudicatory or rulemaking procedure). The proper statutory characterization of this widespread practice is unclear. Because the APA appears to divide all agency actions between rulemaking and adjudication, informal decision-making is often referred to as "informal adjudication." When an agency makes a decision informally, the only procedural requirements are notice of the decision and a brief statement of the reasons for the decision. *See* APA §555(e).

IV. FORMAL ADJUDICATION

Formal adjudication is required "in every case of adjudication required by statute to be determined on the record after opportunity for an agency hearing." APA §554. This is the same predicate for triggering formal rulemaking procedures. The word "hearing" in a statute without a clear indication that that the hearing must be "on the record" is normally insufficient to trigger formal adjudication or formal rulemaking. Absent clear statutory language requiring formal adjudication, the decision of whether to use formal procedures is in the agency's discretion.

CHAPTER 6

APA RULEMAKING PROCEDURES

I. APA §553 INFORMAL ("NOTICE AND COMMENT") RULEMAKING PROCEDURES

A. **Basic Requirements of Informal Rulemaking:** The basic requirements of informal rulemaking are published notice of the proposed rulemaking, opportunity for public comment, and, after consideration of the comments, publication of the final rule together with a concise general statement of the rule's basis and purpose.

B. **Notice:** APA §553 requires notice of either the text of a proposed regulation or a description of the subjects or issues involved in the rulemaking. To guarantee interested parties an opportunity to comment and to prevent agencies from proposing one rule and then promulgating a completely different one, courts have required that the rules ultimately adopted be the logical outgrowth of the proposal, that they not depart substantially from the original proposal, or that the final rule may not materially alter the proposal. The cure for inadequate notice is a new notice and a new comment period.

C. **Meaningful Opportunity to Submit Comments:** Some courts have interpreted APA §553(c)'s requirement that interested parties be allowed to submit comments on proposed rules to require a "meaningful" opportunity to participate. These courts have required agencies to provide notice of any data or studies on which the agency relies. *See Portland Cement Assn. v. Ruckelshaus*, 486 F.2d 375 (D.C. Cir. 1973); *United States v. Nova Scotia Food Prods. Corp.*, 568 F.2d 240 (2d Cir. 1977). Although nothing in the APA explicitly requires it, courts have held that for the opportunity to participate to be meaningful, interested persons must be allowed to respond to opposing comments.

D. **The Problem of Ex Parte Contacts in Rulemaking:** Ex parte contacts consist of communications from interested parties to administrators outside the formalities of the comment process. While such contacts are barred in formal adjudication and formal rulemaking, the APA does not bar ex parte contacts in informal rulemaking.

1. **Ban on ex parte contacts:** While some courts hold that ex parte contacts are generally not barred in informal rulemaking, other courts have ruled that ex parte contacts should not be allowed because they threaten the ability of other interested parties to participate meaningfully in the rulemaking process. Some courts suggest that agencies should consider only the comments presented through the notice-and-comment process because ex parte comments threaten the court's ability, on judicial review, to examine the true basis of agency decisions. Still other courts have confined the ban on ex parte contacts to rulemakings that involve competing private claims to a valuable privilege.

2. **Remedy for ex parte contacts:** Even courts holding that ex parte contacts should not occur recognize that the realities of the political process mean that such contacts may occur. Thus, courts have held that if ex parte contacts do occur, any documents received and a summary of oral communications should be placed on the record.

3. **Intragovernmental ex parte contacts:** The President, as chief executive, has a right to receive information from administrative officials regarding pending rulemakings, and a right to give input on the substance of rulemakings. It may also be appropriate for members of Congress to represent the interests of their constituents through ex parte contacts as long as they do not raise extraneous matters to pressure the agency in the rulemaking process.

E. **Prejudgment in Rulemaking:** A decision-maker in a rulemaking may be disqualified if it is shown by clear and convincing evidence that the decision-maker has prejudged the issues to such a great extent that he or she has an unalterably closed mind, and thus will not consider the comments submitted in the rulemaking process. *See Association of National Advertisers, Inc. v. FTC*, 627 F.2d 1151 (D.C. Cir. 1979).

F. **The Concise General Statement:** APA §553 requires agencies to explain their rules with a "concise general statement of their basis and purpose." The statement must respond to substantial issues raised by the comments and state the agency's views on major issues of law and policy.

G. **Publication of Final Rules:** Agencies must publish final rules in the Federal Register. If a rule is not properly published, the rule is ineffective as to any party without actual notice of the rule. APA §552.

H. **Hybrid Rulemaking:** Some enabling acts impose procedural requirements in addition to those included in §553. They usually consist of discovery, cross-examination of experts, and additional comment periods so that interested parties can comment on adverse comments submitted. Courts also imposed such requirements in complex rulemakings when they viewed §553 procedures as inadequate. In *Vermont Yankee Nuclear Power Corp. v. NRDC*, 435 U.S. 519 (1978), the Supreme Court ruled that courts may not require procedures in addition to those specified in either the APA, another statute, or an enabling act because uncertainty over the correct level of procedure would lead agencies to overproceduralize, losing the benefits of the streamlined rulemaking process. This calls into question judicial imposition of the ban on ex parte communications in rulemakings as well as other judicially imposed procedural requirements.

II. FORMAL RULEMAKING PROCEDURES: THE ADDITIONAL REQUIREMENTS OF APA §§556 AND 557

A. **When Is Formal Rulemaking Required?** Formal rulemaking, which is rulemaking conducted in a formal, adjudicatory procedure, is required when the agency's enabling act requires rules to be made "on the record after opportunity for an agency hearing." Because formal rulemaking is a cumbersome procedure, courts are loath to find that it is required and agencies rarely use it.

B. **Formal Rulemaking Procedures:** Formal rulemaking is conducted like a trial, with an administrative law judge or agency head presiding. Ex parte communications are prohibited. Parties are entitled to present their cases by oral or documentary evidence, and they are entitled to cross-examine opposing witnesses. The record produced at the hearing is the exclusive record for decision in formal rulemaking, and a detailed decision with findings of fact and conclusions of law is required.

III. NEGOTIATED RULEMAKING

Under the Negotiated Rulemaking Act, agencies may formulate proposed rules through a process of formal negotiations among interested parties. If negotiations are successful, the agency normally proposes a rule in line with the negotiated consensus. Such rules are subject to normal notice-and-comment procedures, and the agency is free to change its mind and promulgate a final rule that differs from the rule agreed to in negotiations.

IV. INTERIM FINAL RULES AND DIRECT FINAL RULEMAKING

When time is of the essence, agencies have issued "interim final rules" that go into effect immediately and remain in effect until the rulemaking process is completed. Further, if no adverse comments are expected, some agencies have employed a procedure called "direct final rulemaking" under which an agency publishes a final rule and specifies that it will go into effect unless the agency receives adverse comments. If the agency receives adverse comments, the direct final rulemaking is canceled, and the agency conducts a normal notice-and-comment process. While direct final rulemaking has not been tested in court, it would probably be upheld as a method for promulgating legislative rules as long as the receipt of adverse comments triggers notice-and-comment procedures.

CHAPTER 7

AGENCY ADJUDICATION AND DUE PROCESS

I. ARTICLE III CONSTITUTIONAL LIMITS ON AGENCY ADJUDICATION

Agency adjudication appears to violate Article III's vesting of the judicial power of the United States in the federal courts. However, the federal courts have approved agency adjudication when it occurs under circumstances thought not to threaten the policies and values underlying Article III.

Agency adjudication is most clearly permissible in public rights disputes, which are disputes between a private party and the government over such things as licenses or benefits. More recently, the Supreme Court has approved of agency adjudication of disputes between two private parties where the rights involved arise out of or are closely associated with a federal regulatory scheme, and where the essential attributes of judicial power remain in the federal courts so that the role of the federal courts in the government is not threatened. The Court has found it important that agency orders must be enforced in court, and the parties have a choice between an Article III court and a non-Article III tribunal. Bankruptcy courts may not adjudicate state common-law claims without the consent of the parties. The Court has rejected Justice Brennan's view that non-Article III adjudication is permissible only in the three narrow categories of territorial courts, military courts, and public rights disputes. *See Commodity Futures Trading Commn. v. Schor*, 478 U.S. 833, 859 (1986) (Brennan, J. dissenting).

The Seventh Amendment's reference to "Suits at common law" means that the right to a jury trial attaches to any claim, even one based on a federal statute, that would have been brought before an English common-law court at the time of the framing of the Constitution. In *Securities and Exchange Comm'n v. Jarkesy*, 144 S. Ct. 2117 (2024), the Court held that the defendants in an action brought by the Securities and Exchange Commission (SEC) seeking monetary penalties for alleged securities fraud are entitled to a jury trial because the remedy (civil monetary penalties) and the substance of the claim (fraud) are matters that have historically been adjudicated in courts of law.

II. DUE PROCESS AND THE ADJUDICATORY HEARING

A. **Property Interests:** The first question in any due process dispute is whether the claim involves a protected interest (i.e., life, liberty, or property). While at one time interests such as government benefits were thought of as gratuities that could be withdrawn at any time, today such interests are considered property interests if claims to the benefit are evaluated under a definite set of criteria that create an entitlement to the benefit. The same is true for property interests in government employment, licenses, and permits. *See Board of Regents v. Roth*, 408 U.S. 564 (1972). In the absence of an explicit entitlement, less formal assurances or state practices may create an entitlement.

B. **"Bitter with the Sweet":** In *Arnett v. Kennedy*, 416 U.S. 134 (1974), Justice Rehnquist, joined by two other members of the Court, argued that a civil service employee with a for-cause termination provision (the "sweet") should receive only the minimal process (the "bitter") specified in the statute granting the for-cause entitlement. A majority of the Court rejected this argument, adhering to *Roth*'s separation of procedure from substance.

C. **Liberty:** Some liberty interests are created, like property interests, by external law that creates an entitlement. For example, while prisoners have no constitutional right to parole, if state law creates an entitlement to parole, then a liberty interest is created and due process standards govern the procedures employed at parole hearings. Other liberty interests, such as the rights to freedom of movement and bodily integrity, are recognized as part of the constitutional definition of liberty and are thus created by the Due Process Clause itself.

D. Determining What Process Is Due: How much process is due is determined by applying the *Mathews v. Eldridge* balancing test and asking whether the procedures already provided are adequate. The *Mathews v. Eldridge* balancing test considers (1) the strength of the private interest affected by the government action, (2) the risk of an erroneous deprivation if additional procedure is not afforded, and (3) the government's interest in proceeding with no more process than already afforded. The strongest government interests are those involving collateral consequences of delay rather than simply the cost of the hearing.

Sometimes, alternatives to a trial-like hearing in the agency in advance of the adverse action are held to satisfy due process. These alternatives include common-law remedies, post-deprivation remedies more generally, and a consultative model of procedure. Agencies may not impose legally binding orders on regulated parties without following due process.

E. The Right to a Neutral Decision-maker

1. **Bias:** Due process is violated if a decision-maker has a pecuniary interest in the outcome of the adjudication. Pecuniary interests can be direct, such as a decision-maker who receives a portion of any fines levied in an adjudication, or indirect, such as a decision-maker whose business is in competition with those subject to the agency enforcement. Bias may also exist if a decision-maker feels pressure from agency superiors to decide in a particular way.

2. **Prejudgment:** Due process is violated if it appears that a decision-maker in an adjudication has, in some measure, prejudged the facts or law of a particular case prior to hearing it.

III. STATUTORY HEARING REQUIREMENTS

Many statutes grant the right to a hearing to determine matters such as licenses and government benefits.

A. The Statutorily Required Hearing Must Be Genuine: When a statute grants an applicant a hearing on an application for a government benefit or license, the hearing must provide the applicant with a genuine opportunity to prevail. Under *Ashbacker*, the agency may not make it nearly impossible for the applicant to prevail before holding the hearing. *See Ashbacker Radio Corp. v. FCC*, 326 U.S. 327 (1945).

B. Substantive Standards That Limit Hearings: Agencies with the power to engage in rulemaking may adopt substantive rules that limit the issues addressed at a statutorily prescribed hearing. The rules must be substantively valid. Because these rules are in tension with the party's statutory right to a hearing, courts have required that agencies provide an opportunity for parties to argue that a rule does not, or should not, apply to the particular case.

C. **Applications That Establish Ineligibility:** In *United States v. Storer Broadcasting Co.*, 351 U.S. 192 (1956), the Court held that the Federal Communications Commission (FCC) is free to deny an application without a hearing when the application itself reveals that the license would be denied under a substantively valid statute or regulation.

D. **Procedural Rights in Formal Adjudication:** When formal adjudication applies, APA §§554, 556-557 specify the procedures that agencies must provide. These resemble formal trials. There is no right to discovery, and cross-examination is limited to "such cross-examination as may be required for a full and true disclosure of the fact." APA §556(d). Ex parte contacts are prohibited, and the decision-maker may not be under the supervision of any agency official involved in presenting the case.

E. **The Irrebuttable Presumption Doctrine:** The irrebuttable presumption doctrine held that when there was a liberty or property interest at stake, due process required a hearing on all issues, and a statute could not preclude a hearing on a central issue. This doctrine proved unworkable, and it was abandoned in *Weinberger v. Salfi*, 422 U.S. 749 (1975), when the Court upheld a provision of the Social Security Act that excluded widows who were married to a deceased worker for shorter than nine months from eligibility for survivors' benefits against a challenge that the statute created an irrebuttable presumption that a marriage shorter than nine months was a sham.

CHAPTER 8

SUBSTANTIVE POLICYMAKING IN AGENCIES

I. PERMISSIBLE CONSIDERATIONS IN AGENCY POLICYMAKING

Agencies are required to consider only the factors made relevant by their enabling acts and by other generally applicable statutes such as the National Environmental Policy Act (NEPA). In *Massachusetts v. EPA*, 549 U.S. 497 (2007), the Court made clear that agencies should consider only those factors identified in relevant statutes. Agencies should make policy by applying their expertise, in a reasoned fashion, to the factors made statutorily relevant. Agencies should not take factors into account that are not within the considerations made relevant by statute or valid regulation.

II. COST-BENEFIT ANALYSIS

Cost-benefit analysis promotes reasoned decision-making by forcing agencies to quantify the effects of their actions in a more concrete fashion. While it has been argued that agencies should be required to conduct cost-benefit analysis regarding their major policy decisions and should not adopt a policy unless the benefits outweigh the costs, courts will not mandate cost-benefit analysis unless it is statutorily required. While courts previously have not read standards such as "reasonably necessary or appropriate" as requiring cost-benefit analysis, perhaps because many costs and benefits are difficult to quantify, the Supreme Court has recently been more likely to read such language as requiring or at least allowing cost-benefit analysis. For example, *Michigan v. EPA,* 576 U.S. 743 (2015) held that the Clean Air Act's phrase "if the Administrator finds such regulation is appropriate and necessary" requires consideration of costs. Sometimes the argument for cost-benefit analysis is rejected because Congress appears to prefer values other than efficiency in many regulatory programs. Agencies may voluntarily use cost-benefit analysis under such statutes unless other statutory language prohibits it.

III. IMPACT STATEMENTS

Another method of forcing agencies to focus on the effects of their actions is to require the agency to prepare an impact statement, such as an environmental impact statement or a small business regulatory impact statement. Impact statements improve decision-making and provide an opportunity for opponents of the agency's plan to put pressure on the agency to change or abandon its plans due to undesirable effects.

A. **Environmental Impact Statements Under NEPA:** NEPA requires federal agencies to prepare environmental impact statements (EIS) regarding "major Federal actions significantly affecting the quality of the human environment." The EIS must detail the effects and include consideration of alternatives.

B. **Environmental Effects:** In addition to traditional environmental effects, NEPA covers a broad range of effects on the human environment, such as displacement of social institutions and concentration of low-income residents in a neighborhood. For NEPA to apply, there must be a physical alteration of the environment and the matter must be within the agency's control.

C. **NEPA Is Essentially Procedural:** The EIS must be part of the record during agency consideration of its action, and courts have held that the agency must consider the environmental effects. Nothing in NEPA, however, requires that agency action be changed or abandoned due to environmental effects. Judicial review of the adequacy of the EIS is deferential.

IV. CONSISTENCY AND CLARITY REQUIREMENTS

Courts have, on judicial review, required agencies to operate under clearly stated substantive criteria and have required agencies to treat like cases alike.

A. **Clarity:** The clarity cases, which are in tension with decisions allowing agencies the discretion to decide issues on a case-by-case basis, hold that agency action may be taken only pursuant to clear criteria. Some courts have held that where property or liberty interests are at stake, clarity is required by due process.

B. **Agency Decisions Are Judged on the Reasons Stated by the Agency:** Related to the clarity requirement is the well-established doctrine that agency decisions are evaluated, on judicial review, based on the reasons given by the agency at the time the decision was made, not on reasons first offered on judicial review. Related to this, the agency must rely on the true reasons for its actions, not on reasons that the record demonstrates are pretextual. *Department of Commerce v. New York*, 588 U.S. 752 (2019).

C. **Consistency:** Agencies are required to be consistent (i.e., to treat like cases alike) and must offer an explanation when they treat like cases differently.

D. **Agencies Must Follow Their Own Rules:** Agencies are required to follow their own formally adopted rules, whether those rules have been adopted in a rulemaking proceeding or announced in the course of an agency adjudication, unless the agency has validly changed its rule. Agencies must apply their rules as written and may not apply a rule in a manner inconsistent with the rule as written. *See Allentown Mack Sales and Service, Inc. v. NLRB*, 522 U.S. 359 (1998). However, courts often allow agencies to ignore rules that have not been formally adopted in a rulemaking or adjudication.

E. **Estoppel and Administrative Agencies:** Except in extreme circumstances and where government funds are not involved, agencies are not estopped by the conduct or statements of agency officials. For example, if an agency official gives erroneous advice by misstating the eligibility requirements for a government program, the erroneous advice does not estop the agency from relying on the program's actual requirements to deny claims. Nonmutual collateral estoppel does not apply against the government.

F. **Nonacquiescence:** Agencies sometimes refuse to acquiesce to legal rulings by lower federal courts. In such cases, the agency may follow the ruling in the circuit in which it was rendered but will adhere to its position in other courts with the possibility of prevailing with a favorable ruling in the Supreme Court. While intercircuit nonacquiescence seems appropriate in some circumstances, intracircuit nonacquiescence, in which an agency refuses to follow a decision of the court of appeals even within the circuit that rendered the decision, is difficult to defend.

CHAPTER 9

AGENCY ENFORCEMENT AND LICENSING

I. ENFORCEMENT DISCRETION

A. **Decisions Not to Prosecute or Regulate:** Unless an enabling act contains standards under which an agency is required to take enforcement action against a violator, a decision not to prosecute is not reviewable. By and large, courts have concluded that the agency should be left to decide, in its expert judgment, which enforcement actions present the best use of agency resources.

B. **Potential Problems with Agency Enforcement Discretion:** Unreviewable agency enforcement discretion presents the potential for subversion of congressional intent by applying different priorities than those that led Congress to pass the agency's enabling act. Agency prosecutorial discretion may allow an agency to play political favorites and may also lead the agency to select only easy targets for prosecution, leaving serious violations unaddressed.

C. **Discriminatory Enforcement:** Subjects of agency enforcement sometimes claim that although they may have violated regulatory norms, the agency should not issue an enforcement order against them unless and until the agency issues enforcement orders against others (for example, competitors) engaged in the same practice. The standard for deciding whether a court should preclude an agency from enforcing an order until the agency orders others in the industry to halt the same practice is "patent abuse of discretion"—a very difficult standard to meet. As long as an agency can articulate a rational basis for its actions, the order will be enforced.

D. **Discriminatory Imposition of Sanctions:** Agencies are free to impose whatever sanctions are within their statutory authority. Courts have rejected claims that agencies have imposed overly harsh sanctions for violations, either when compared to sanctions imposed on others, or under agency policy regarding sanctions.

E. **Constitutionally Based Claims of Discriminatory Enforcement:** An agency violates equal protection if it selects its enforcement targets based on a suspect classification. *See Yick Wo v. Hopkins*, 118 U.S. 356 (1886). When outspoken criticism of an agency or the program the agency administers triggers enforcement, regulated parties have unsuccessfully argued that the prosecution punishes or chills speech in violation of the First Amendment.

II. LICENSING AND RATEMAKING

A. **Occupational Licensing:** Doctors, lawyers, optometrists, pharmacists, hair stylists, truck drivers, and many other professionals must obtain licenses from the state in order to practice their professions.

1. **Licenses are property protected by due process:** Because discernible standards normally govern the grant, denial, renewal, and revocation of professional and business licenses, such licenses are protected by due process as property.

2. **Bias due to self-interest and the problem of self-regulation:** Occupational licensing often presents the potential for bias due to self-interest because the licensing board may be dominated by one segment of a profession that seeks to avoid competition from another segment. If the members of the board have an interest in the outcome of a disciplinary proceeding before it, due process may preclude them from hearing it.

B. **Business Licensing Procedures:** In general, federal and state law provides license applicants with formal adjudicatory procedures at some point in the process before an application for a business or professional license is finally denied.

1. **"Public interest" standard for granting broadcast licenses:** Broadcast licensing is studied more often than other forms of licensing. The FCC decides whether to grant a broadcast license based on the very discretionary standard of public interest, convenience, and necessity.

2. **Broadcast licensing hearing requirements:** The FCC is required to hold a full adjudicatory hearing before rejecting an application for a broadcast license.

3. **Mutually exclusive applications: The *Ashbacker* rule:** When two applicants file competing applications, the FCC may not grant one of the applications without holding a hearing on the other. *See Ashbacker Radio Corp. v. FCC*, 326 U.S. 327 (1945). To meet this obligation, the FCC would hold a comparative hearing in which the relative merits of applicants are judged on a variety of factors such as diversification of ownership, involvement of ownership in the management of the station, the quality of proposed programming, and the character of the applicants. While comparative hearings were formerly held on renewal applications, statutory reform has created an entitlement to renewal absent inferior service or other violations by the incumbent licensee.

4. **Restricting the scope of hearings by rule: *Storer*:** In *United States v. Storer Broadcasting Co.*, 351 U.S. 192 (1956), the Court held that the FCC may make the "public interest, convenience, and necessity" standard more specific with rules, such as multiple ownership rules that restrict the number of stations owned by a licensee. The Court held that it did not violate the right to a full hearing to deny a license based on noncompliance with an FCC rule.

C. **Ratemaking Principles and Procedures:** Ratemaking is the procedure for setting rates in regulated industries such as electric power and telephone service. Ratemaking has been conducted according to three different models: one in which rates set by the company are subject to challenge as "unreasonable," one in which rates are prescribed in a comprehensive formal ratemaking process, and one in which the company files tariffs that are barely examined by the agency unless someone challenges them. A tariff is essentially a schedule of rates and services. The Supreme Court has rejected the FCC's effort to de-tariff most long-distance telephone companies, ruling that the tariff-filing requirement was the heart of the regulatory scheme. *MCI v. AT&T*, 512 U.S. 218 (1994).

CHAPTER 10

AGENCY INFORMATION GATHERING

I. INSPECTIONS

Many agencies monitor compliance with regulatory requirements by inspecting the subjects of regulation. To do so, the agency must have authority to inspect. Further, agencies are subject to constitutional constraints on information gathering.

A. **Administrative Authority to Inspect Regulated Businesses:** The APA prohibits agencies from conducting inspections, or otherwise gathering information, without legal authority. APA §555(c).

B. **Constitutional Constraints on Agency Inspection:** Agency inspections are subject to constitutional constraints, most notably those imposed by the Fourth Amendment.

However, probable cause (in the criminal law sense) is not required for warrants to conduct inspections. In "pervasively regulated businesses," warrants may be unnecessary.

1. **Normally, a warrant is required:** Under normal circumstances, a warrant is required before government agents may enter and inspect a business to monitor compliance with regulatory requirements.

2. **Warrants for administrative inspections may issue without probable cause:** An agency may obtain a warrant merely by showing that normal legislative or administrative standards for conducting an inspection are met. The agency does not need probable cause in the criminal law sense. Rather, probable cause for an administrative warrant is established merely by showing that the inspection is pursuant to reasonable legislative or administrative standards This rule seems contrary to the spirit of the Fourth Amendment, which requires probable cause for all warrants.

3. **Pervasively regulated businesses:** No warrant is required to inspect the premises of businesses that are subject to pervasive regulation, such as junkyards, firearms dealers, pawnshops, businesses that serve alcohol, and mines.

C. **Regulatory Inspections of Homes:** Recipients of government benefits may be required to allow welfare caseworkers to inspect their homes as a condition of continued benefits. Also, warrants to inspect a home for compliance with a building code do not require probable cause in the criminal sense. Rather, warrants may issue if the agency establishes that the inspection is part of its normal regulatory scheme to monitor compliance with the relevant code. Finally, probation officers may, without a warrant or probable cause, search the homes of convicted criminals who have been placed on probation.

D. **Drug Testing:** Drug testing programs are evaluated according to several factors, including the expectation of privacy of the individual tested, the degree to which the testing program invades that privacy, the importance of the governmental interest underlying the testing program, and the degree to which the testing program's standards ameliorate the potential for arbitrary selection of individuals to be tested.

II. PRODUCTION OF INFORMATION AND DOCUMENTS

A. **Agency Requests for Information or Documents:** An agency may require regulated parties to provide information or documents as long as the demand is not too indefinite or burdensome, and the information sought is reasonably relevant to a matter of legitimate agency concern. Subjects of investigations normally cannot test the strength of an agency's case or agency's jurisdiction in a proceeding to enforce a subpoena.

B. **Disclosure of Privileged Information or Trade Secrets:** It is unclear whether federal agencies must respect state law privileges such as the attorney-client privilege, the doctor-patient privilege, and the marital privilege. Corporations, other entities (such as labor unions and partnerships), and the custodians of records for such entities, have no Fifth Amendment privilege against providing the government with information or documents. The government may be required, under the Takings Clause, to compensate a regulated party whose trade secret information is disclosed.

III. THE PAPERWORK REDUCTION ACT

Before an agency may promulgate a new request for information, the agency must submit a proposal to the Office of Information and Regulatory Affairs (OIRA) within the Office of Management and Budget (OMB). OIRA may reject the agency's proposal if it finds that the agency does not have a legitimate need for the information. The Paperwork Reduction Act (PRA) does not apply to disclosure rules, i.e., requirements that one regulated party disclose information directly to another party.

CHAPTER 11

PRIVATE ENFORCEMENT OF REGULATORY NORMS AND PREEMPTION

I. THE CITIZENS' SUIT

A. Suits Against Violators: Citizens' suit provisions typically authorize "any citizen" or "any person" to seek damages, an injunction, or both against violations of the relevant statute by private parties and by government. This citizens' suit provision does not authorize a suit against the government for regulatory errors but only for conduct that violates the substance of a regulatory program, such as pollution by the government in violation of an environmental statute.

B. Suits against the Government as Regulator: Citizens' suit provisions typically provide for actions in the nature of mandamus against regulators when it is alleged that they have failed to perform nondiscretionary regulatory duties. This provision is not a substitute for judicial review and may not be used to examine the substance of discretionary agency action.

C. Standing Problems in Citizens' Suits: Plaintiffs in citizens' suits must meet all Article III standing requirements. Citizens' suit provisions may, however, overrule prudential limits on standing and place all "citizens" within the zone of interests of the relevant regulatory program.

II. IMPLIED PRIVATE RIGHTS OF ACTION

If congressional intent to do so exists, a federal court may imply a right of action from a regulatory statute so that a private party can sue another private party for violating the regulatory or criminal statute even if the statute itself provides only for enforcement by a federal agency or criminal prosecution. Contrary to older cases, the recent cases allow rights of action to be implied only if it appears that Congress intended courts to do so. The focus on congressional intent arises from concerns that those courts that implied rights of action without evidence of such intent were usurping Congress's legislative function.

III. ALTERNATIVE STATE REMEDIES AND REGULATORY PREEMPTION

A. **Preemption of State Remedies:** Preemption means that federal law overrides state law. There is a presumption, rooted in federalism concerns, that state law is not preempted unless Congress's intent to do so is clear. Nonetheless, Congress may preempt state law, including state tort products liability law, when the product is also regulated by a federal agency.

1. **Express preemption:** Under express preemption, Congress preempts state law explicitly, by providing in a statute that state law is preempted.

2. **Implied preemption:** Sometimes federal law implicitly preempts state law. There are three kinds of implied preemption: field preemption (when federal law is so comprehensive it appears that Congress must have intended to displace state law that is within the "field" occupied by Congress), conflict preemption (when state and federal law actually conflict), and obstacle preemption (when state law stands as an obstacle to the realization of federal policy). Obstacle preemption is controversial because it leaves federal courts with a great deal of discretion to preempt state law without clear indications of congressional intent to do so.

B. **The Primary Jurisdiction Doctrine:** The primary jurisdiction doctrine requires that a claim within the substantive jurisdiction of an agency must be heard first by that agency even if the facts give rise to a claim otherwise cognizable in a court. A savings clause in a regulatory statute may prevent the primary jurisdiction doctrine from operating.

CHAPTER 12

LIABILITY OF AGENCIES AND OFFICIALS

I. SOVEREIGN IMMUNITY AND SUITS AGAINST FEDERAL AGENTS AND AGENCIES

A. **Common-Law Sovereign Immunity:** At common law, sovereign immunity barred damages actions against the government and government officials acting in their official capacities unless the government consented to the suit.

B. **The Federal Torts Claim Act:** The Federal Tort Claims Act (FTCA) waives the sovereign immunity of the federal government for negligent or otherwise wrongful acts or omissions by the United States government or its employees. The FTCA creates federal government liability for "tort claims, . . . in the same manner and to the same extent as a private individual under like circumstances." 28 U.S.C. §2674. The FTCA is often used to pursue an action for damages when the conduct of administrators is allegedly tortious. Strict liability is not allowed.

C. **Exceptions to FTCA Liability:** The FTCA contains numerous exceptions and limitations, the most important of which is the discretionary-function exception. The Supreme Court has defined the discretionary-function exception as exempting actions from liability when the official has a choice and when the action involves the "permissible exercise of policy judgment." In addition to law and policymaking functions, the courts have held that the discretionary-functions exception bars liability for errors in the planning stages of government operations. The Court has also been very skeptical of claims that the government should be held liable for negligence in performing inspections and similar regulatory functions.

D. **The *Feres* Doctrine:** The Supreme Court has created a nonstatutory exception to the FTCA, called the "*Feres* doctrine," for military activities. This doctrine basically bars all claims that are "incident to service" in the armed forces.

E. **Exclusive Remedy:** If the FTCA applies, government liability is exclusive and the individual official may not be held liable. However, if an exception to the FTCA applies, such as the discretionary-function exception, then a claim against the individual official may be brought.

II. LIABILITY OF INDIVIDUAL FEDERAL OFFICIALS

A. **Common-law Immunities of Government Officials:** In many situations, government officials are privileged to engage in conduct that, if performed by a private party, would be tortious. The courts have also recognized immunity from tort liability for federal government officials acting within the scope of their duties. Further, if a claim against a federal government official falls within the scope of the FTCA, the government is substituted as defendant, and the individual official is released from liability.

B. **Judicially Created Constitutional Tort Liability:** The Supreme Court, in *Bivens v. Six Unknown Named Agents of Federal Bureau of Narcotics*, 403 U.S. 388 (1971), created a damages action against federal officials for constitutional torts. Each extension of *Bivens* to a new constitutional right is evaluated for whether it makes policy sense to recognize a cause of action.

1. **Exceptions to *Bivens:*** The *Bivens* action is not available when there are "special factors counseling hesitation in the absence of affirmative action by Congress," or when Congress has provided an alternative remedy that it explicitly declared to be a *substitute* for the *Bivens* action. The existence of a comprehensive alternative remedial scheme has been considered a special factor counseling hesitation. More recent cases hold that separation of powers concerns counsel against extending *Bivens* to new contexts.

2. **Immunities in *Bivens* actions:** Administrative officials performing judicial, legislative, and prosecutorial functions are absolutely immune from damages because at common law, judges, legislators, and prosecutors were absolutely immune from damages. Officials performing functions not traditionally accorded an absolute immunity are protected by a qualified immunity. A plaintiff can overcome the qualified immunity by showing that the defendant violated a clearly established constitutional right of which a reasonable official should have known.

III. LIABILITY OF STATE AND LOCAL GOVERNMENT OFFICIALS

State and local government officials can be sued in federal court under 42 U.S.C. §1983 for damages and injunctive relief for conduct violating the federal Constitution and laws.

A. **Eleventh Amendment:** The Eleventh Amendment, as interpreted and applied by the Supreme Court, prohibits the federal courts from awarding damages against states and state government agencies. State officials can be enjoined from violating federal law and state officials can be held personally liable for damages, to be paid out of their own pockets. States are immune from §1983 damages in state court as well.

B. **"And Laws" Actions:** Section 1983 provides a cause of action against state officials who violate federal statutory law. However, when the federal statute contains a comprehensive remedial scheme that includes its own private right of action against violations, the Supreme Court has held that plaintiffs must use the particular statutory remedy and not the more general §1983 action. The Court has also held that the §1983 remedy for violating a federal statute is not available when the federal statute creates no enforceable rights, for example, when the statute's only substantive requirement is a vague "reasonable efforts" standard.

C. **Immunities:** Defendants in §1983 actions are protected by the same immunities that the courts have applied in *Bivens* actions.

D. **Municipal Liability:** Municipalities are "persons" subject to suit under §1983, but they may be held liable only for municipal policy or custom and may not be held liable on a vicarious liability theory for the constitutional violations of their employees.

CHAPTER 13

FREEDOM OF INFORMATION AND OPEN MEETINGS

I. THE FREEDOM OF INFORMATION ACT (FOIA)

A. **Public Right of Access to Agency Records:** FOIA requires that agencies allow public inspection, upon request, of all agency "records" unless the records sought fall within one of FOIA's exceptions.

1. **Agency records:** Agency records are those records that are created or obtained by the agency in the course of doing the agency's work and in the control of the agency at the time of the FOIA request.

2. **Records "wrongfully withheld":** FOIA creates a legal claim when an agency "wrongfully withholds" agency records.

3. **Special FOIA definition of "agency":** The FOIA definition of "agency" includes entities that may not be subject to other APA requirements, such as government corporations and executive branch entities that may collect information, but have no power to take actions having any legal effect.

B. **Exceptions to FOIA:** FOIA contains nine categories of exceptions to the requirement that agencies disclose their records. *See* 5 U.S.C. §552(b)(1)-(9). The Supreme Court has stated repeatedly that FOIA exceptions should be narrowly construed. The exceptions include classified national defense and foreign policy records; records concerning agency personnel matters; privileged or confidential business or financial records; trade secrets; privileged or confidential commercial information; law enforcement records where disclosure would harm law enforcement efforts; internal agency memoranda; personnel, medical, or law enforcement records where disclosure would unduly invade privacy; and records protected against disclosure by any other statute.

C. **Disclosure of Exempt Records:** Nothing in FOIA precludes an agency from voluntarily turning over records that FOIA exceptions would allow the agency to withhold. However, the Trade Secrets Act makes it a criminal offense for a government official to release information held to be within the FOIA trade-secrets exception. A person whose confidential information is threatened to be released by an agency has a "reverse-FOIA" cause of action under the APA's judicial review provisions (not the Trade Secrets Act itself) to prevent disclosure.

D. **The Privacy Act of 1974:** The Privacy Act of 1974, 5 U.S.C. §552a, prohibits agencies from disclosing records "except pursuant to a written request by, or with the prior consent of, the individual to whom the record pertains." The Privacy Act also restricts the information agencies are allowed to collect on individuals. The Privacy Act's nondisclosure provisions do not apply to records required to be disclosed under FOIA.

II. DISCOVERY FROM THE GOVERNMENT IN LITIGATION

Another method of obtaining government records is to request them in discovery during litigation. The government has two special privileges that protect government records from discovery in litigation: evidentiary privilege and executive immunity (also known as executive privilege).

A. **Evidentiary Privileges:** Evidentiary privileges protect records in sensitive categories like state secrets, military secrets, and sensitive foreign affairs matters. The court determines whether the material sought in discovery is protected by a privilege by balancing the litigant's need for the information against the government's interest in secrecy.

B. Executive Immunity: When the executive branch claims immunity from the discovery process, the court balances the executive branch's need for confidentiality against the litigant's need for the material. When the President invokes executive privilege, the burden is on the party seeking discovery to demonstrate that the material is essential to justice.

IV. OPEN-MEETINGS REQUIREMENTS

A. The Sunshine Act: The Government in the Sunshine Act, 5 U.S.C. §552b, requires all agencies (using FOIA's definition of "agency") that are headed by a "collegial body composed of two or more individual members," to announce their meetings at least one week in advance and to open those meetings to the public, unless a Sunshine Act exception applies. Agencies headed by a single individual are not subject to the Sunshine Act, even when the head of the agency meets with subordinates to discuss agency business.

1. **"Meeting of an agency":** A gathering of agency members is a "meeting of an agency" within the Sunshine Act if the members "jointly conduct or dispose of agency business." The Sunshine Act does not apply to meetings that are purely consultative in character when the agency does not purport to conduct business.

2. **When may an agency meet in private?** The Sunshine Act contains ten categories of exceptions to its open-meetings requirement, most of which track the exceptions to FOIA's disclosure requirements. *See* 5 U.S.C. §552b(c)(l)-(8). A meeting may be closed pursuant to the Sunshine Act exceptions only by a public vote of a majority of the members of the agency.

B. The Federal Advisory Committee Act (FACA): FACA requires presidential advisory committees, which include private citizens as members, to comply with the Sunshine Act with regard to their meetings and with FOIA with regard to their records. Because it interferes with the President's ability to seek advice from private citizens, it has been argued that FACA violates the separation of powers.

EXAM TIPS

EXAM TIPS

SUMMARY OF CONTENTS

Exam Tips on INTRODUCTION TO STUDYING ADMINISTRATIVE LAW

Sources of law

- Here are some important issues to keep in mind in connection with any administrative law exam: You should be clear on an exam about the ***source of the law*** that is relevant to the issues. Be explicit about when you are drawing on the ***Constitution***, the ***APA***, the ***particular agency's statute or rules***, some ***other statute***, or ***traditional common-law*** principles.
- Whenever an issue arises regarding agency power to act, look carefully at and draw on the agency's ***enabling act.***
- Whether an agency is located in an executive branch department or is an independent agency may be important to understanding the legal and policy issues raised by an administrative law exam.

Public choice and public interest theories

- The political background often helps understand agency action.
  - If, under public choice theory, it appears that an agency was ***captured*** by a powerful interest group, you might express skepticism about the agency's actions.
  - On the other hand, if it appears agency experts are pursuing an important ***public policy goal***, you might argue for deference to the agency.
- It is important to be cognizant of the fact that administrative law has evolved significantly under the Roberts Court and that this includes changes to some administrative law fundamentals. Thus, on an exam, it is important to think about whether recent changes may require more creative analysis than is typical on a law school exam.

Exam Tips on SEPARATION OF POWERS AND DISTRIBUTION OF ADMINISTRATIVE POWER

Nondelegation

- In nondelegation doctrine issues, it often is useful to address the history of the doctrine and explain how it has evolved from a strict, categorical approach to the current intelligible principle standard.
  - Point out that the nondelegation doctrine is a very lenient standard and that no statute has failed the intelligible principle test in recent years. Mention the

Whitman case as the most recent example. However, it may also be helpful to note that the intelligible principle test is under attack and may be replaced by a more stringent standard.

☞ If a question calls for an extended discussion of the nondelegation doctrine, it is helpful to ground that discussion in Justice Rehnquist's analysis in his *Benzene* concurrence of the normative bases for the doctrine, most importantly that Congress makes the basic policy choices.

☞ It also may be useful to discuss the nondelegation doctrine in light of larger separation of powers concerns such as those raised in Justice Scalia's dissent in *Mistretta v. United States*, 488 U.S. 361 (1989).

Separation of powers

☛ In all separation of powers questions, start the discussion by identifying and applying any relevant constitutional provisions, such as the bicameralism and presentment clauses with regard to the legislative veto or the Appointments Clause in appointment and removal cases. Then go on to discuss more general separation of powers concerns that arise in cases involving issues such as the legislative veto, appointment and removal powers, presidential control, and the like.

Appointment and removal

☛ In many appointment and removal cases, it is important to understand the remedy—sometimes the Court prohibits an official from exercising a power instead of holding that the method of appointment or removal was unconstitutional.

☞ For example, point out that any official appointed by or removable by Congress cannot exercise powers reserved to "officers of the United States" since "officers of the United States" only may be appointed in accordance with the Appointments Clause and may not be removed by Congress.

☞ If relevant, mention that Congress may appoint and remove its own officials.

☞ With regard to appointments made by someone other than the President or by the President without Senate advice and consent, examine whether the official being appointed is an inferior officer under *Morrison* and *Edmond v. United States*, 520 U.S. 651 (1997), and whether the appointing entity is a department head or court of law.

☛ In cases involving Congress's power to restrict the President's power to remove executive officials, in addition to analyzing the issue in light of Congress's broad power to restrict removal that the Court recognized in *Morrison v. Olson*, it is important to note that the Court's attitude toward removal restrictions has evolved into a more skeptical view of restrictions on the President's power to manage the executive branch. While a discussion of the "quasi-legislative" and "quasi-judicial" language of *Humphrey's Executor v. United States*, 295 U.S. 602 (1935), might be appropriate, *Morrison* better represents current law.

- In questions involving removal restrictions, watch for multilevel for-cause restrictions, under which the official can be removed only for cause by an official that the President may not remove without cause. If this occurs, invoke the *PCAOB* separation of powers rule against this sort of arrangement and then consider whether there is a reason for an exception to the rule, for example if the official performs an adjudicatory function or is a low-level employee.

Constitutionality of agency adjudication

- When discussing the constitutionality of locating adjudication within administrative agencies, be sure to explore the different treatment accorded public rights and private rights, and be sure to analyze the issue in light of the factors stated in *CFTC v. Schor*, including that the agency adjudication occurs in a particularized area of law related to a regulatory scheme, that orders are enforceable only in court, that effective judicial review is available, and that the essence of the judicial power is not delegated to the agency. Further, if the claim before the agency resembles a traditional common-law type of claim, discuss whether *Jarkesy* entitles private litigants to a jury trial, which would make agency adjudication improper

---

Exam Tips on THE AVAILABILITY OF JUDICIAL REVIEW OF ADMINISTRATIVE DECISIONS

Jurisdiction vs. reviewability

- Be sure to keep the issues of jurisdiction and reviewability separate. You are more likely to be asked about reviewability than about jurisdiction.
  - If jurisdiction is an issue, mention the old "rule of thumb" and then explain that jurisdiction depends more on what court has jurisdiction by statute than on any rule of thumb.
  - Point out that the Supreme Court favors jurisdiction in the court of appeals for reasons of judicial economy, and thus if there is a statute that can be construed to give jurisdiction to that court, the Supreme Court will probably read it to do so.

General reviewability issues

- When discussing whether an agency action is reviewable, be sure to discuss whether the action is final, whether there are any ripeness problems, and whether either subsection of APA §701(a) affects reviewability.
  - However, if the action is obviously reviewable, don't waste time discussing reviewability in depth — it is probably not being asked about.

Statutory preclusion of review

- For statutory preclusion of review, be sure to look for both explicit and implicit preclusion.
- If there is statutory preclusion, be sure to evaluate whether the particular action over which review is sought is within the scope of the precluding statute.
  - If the statute precludes review of particular decisions such as a denial of government benefits, analyze whether the party seeking judicial review is challenging the type of decision specified in the statute, or whether the party seeking judicial review is challenging something else, such as the way the entire program is being administered.
  - In cases involving global challenges to the way an entire program is being administered, point out that although *Southern Utah Wilderness Alliance* indicates that such review should not be allowed, the Court in the *McNary* decision seems open to arguments that global challenges are not precluded by statutes disallowing review of individual denials of benefits.

Committed to agency discretion by law

- In evaluating whether an action is committed to agency discretion by law, be sure to look for all three ways in which that can happen: no law to apply, a deeming clause, and a category traditionally not subject to judicial review.
- Make clear that these three understandings are related, that each tends to support the other, and that all involve evidence that Congress did not intend to subject the agency action to review.
- Look for arguments that the challenged agency action is akin to prosecutorial discretion. If it is, analyze reviewability under that line of cases (i.e., analyze whether there are clear standards requiring agency enforcement).
- Remember that there is serious doubt about whether review of constitutional issues may be barred.

Standing

- Be sure the party seeking to challenge agency action has standing. Look for injury, causation, redressability, zone of interests, and the prudential limitations. Since the precedent in this area appears inconsistent, marshal arguments from both sides to show that you understand the issues even if the conclusion is not obvious.
- When the party seeking to challenge agency action is not the regulated party, be sure to discuss the zone of interests test and how it differs from the legal rights test.
  - If there is a citizens' suit provision, point out that everyone given permission to sue under that provision is probably within the zone of interests.
  - In cases arising under statutes other than the APA, point out that the zone of interests test might not apply, since the zone of interests test may be based on the language of APA §702.

- Also, look for redressability problems—will the court be able to provide an effective remedy? If the injury is procedural only, point out that the redressability requirement might not be as strictly enforced as in other cases.
- Recall that the prudential limitations, including the ban on asserting the rights of third parties and the ban on litigating a generalized grievance, are subject to override by Congress.
  - Look for override, such as by a citizen suit provision.
  - Remember, however, that Congress may not override constitutional standing doctrines.

Ripeness and exhaustion

- Ripeness questions often arise when it appears that the agency's consideration is not complete. A common ripeness issue is whether a court should review a regulation before the agency has tried to enforce it. Use the *Abbott Labs* ***fitness*** and ***hardship*** tests. The differences between *Abbott Labs* and *Gardner v. Toilet Goods Association, Inc.*, 387 U.S. 158 (1967), are useful in applying the fitness and hardship test.
- An attempt to force an agency to act may raise ripeness questions. If you are asked whether an agency can be compelled to act, be sure to address whether the agency's failure to act is ripe.
  - Agency inaction, as in a refusal to act, may not be ripe for review if the agency is still deciding whether to act, although there may be a factual argument that the agency has delayed so long that its delay amounts to a decision not to act.
  - If an agency denies a petition to make a rule, the denial is final and subject to review, but only under a very deferential standard.
- If exhaustion of administrative remedies is an issue, apply the factors from *McCarthy v. Madigan*, 503 U.S. 140 (1992). However, if the case is brought under the APA, point out that under *Darby*, those factors may not apply and the only issue may be whether a statute or regulation requires that certain remedies be exhausted.

Exam Tips on *JUDICIAL REVIEW OF ADMINISTRATIVE ACTION*

Standards of review

- Always look carefully at APA §706 to determine which standard of review applies to the particular agency action challenged.
  - If the predicates for substantial evidence review (agency decision under formal procedures or "on the record after hearing") are present, substantial evidence review applies. In a close case, it might be useful to spend time analyzing whether substantial evidence review applies.

- ☞ De novo review is rarely available and not likely to be on an exam. However, if it appears that a predicate for de novo review is present, be sure to state the grounds — where agency adjudicatory fact-finding procedures are inadequate and where new factual issues arise in an action to enforce nonadjudicatory agency action — and be sure to explain that under de novo review, the reviewing court makes a fresh determination of the facts subject to de novo review.
- ☞ If no predicate for either substantial evidence review or de novo review is present, use the arbitrary and capricious test, and explain that this test always applies since it has no predicate.

- ☛ When applying any standard of review, remember that under APA §706, the court looks at the ***whole record***, not just those parts of the record that support the agency. Thus, if an exam calls for review of a particular agency action, be sure to address the complete record.

- ☛ The substantial evidence test applies to formal adjudication and formal rulemaking done under §§556 and 557 or otherwise "on the record after hearing."
  - ☞ Point out that except where §§556 and 557 are specified, courts rarely find that substantial evidence review applies — the hearing must truly be "on the record" in the sense of a formal adjudicatory-type hearing.
  - ☞ If the substantial evidence test applies, state the definition of the test ("such relevant evidence as a reasonable mind might accept as adequate to support a conclusion"), and be sure to look at the whole record and discuss whether the evidence against the agency's decision substantially outweighs the evidence on the other side.

Issues of law

- ☛ On issues of law, remember that *Chevron* has been overruled and *Loper-Bright* instructs reviewing courts to independently determine the best meaning of the statute. However, after applying the tools of statutory interpretation, it is also important to raise the possibility of deference under the *Skidmore* factors if the statute is lacking in clear congressional intent.

- ☛ Watch for situations in which the major questions doctrine applies because the agency has found a new power in an old statute, has issued rules with massive economic implications or with implications for an ongoing political controversy, or has newly entered an area of traditional state authority.

Arbitrary and capricious

- ☛ On issues subject to arbitrary and capricious review, be sure to state the standard as laid down in *Overton Park* and then apply the test to the issues at hand.
  - ☞ Be sure that the agency applied the correct legal standard, considered all relevant factors, considered alternatives, and explained its decision adequately, which includes stating conclusions on the major issues raised.

- When grounds for setting aside agency action exist, discuss the appropriate remedy— should the court remand the issue to the agency for further consideration, should the court allow the agency to supplement the record, or should the court simply rule that the agency may not do what it proposes? If a court issues a nationwide injunction, it might be helpful to discuss the propriety of such orders.

Exam Tips on AGENCY CHOICE OF PROCEDURAL MODE

Rulemaking vs. adjudication

- As is the case in many areas in administrative law, look for relevant APA sections first, and make sure to apply them to the exam question.
  - Recall although the APA requires adjudication for an agency to issue an order and rulemaking to issue a rule, it does not state when agencies must use one process or another for policymaking, so in a question regarding the choice between rulemaking and adjudication, stress the discretionary nature of the decision.
  - Consult the definitions in APA §551, and note that if an agency wants to issue an order, it must use adjudication, and if it wants to issue an actual rule, it must use rulemaking.
- In questions involving whether due process requires a hearing, be sure to discuss whether the administrative action affects a small number of parties based on their special characteristics.
  - The discussion here may benefit from pointing out the distinction between legislative and adjudicative facts. It is often useful to discuss whether the hypothetical is more like *Londoner* or *Bi-Metallic*.
  - If the agency finding is based on adjudicative facts, perhaps adjudication is required.
  - If the agency finding is based on legislative facts, a rulemaking process may be sufficient.
- In discussing whether an agency has power to use rulemaking, extol the policy virtues of rulemaking, since those virtues seem important when courts broadly construe grants of rulemaking authority.
- On the other side, discuss how rulemaking may detract from a party's right to a hearing, and how rulemaking may be contrary to Congress's intent for primarily adjudicatory agencies.
- If a party's argument is that adjudication is required simply by the appearance of the word "hearing" in the agency's statute, point out that the courts have not interpreted the

word hearing alone to require adjudicatory procedures and that an agency's interpretation of "hearing" might receive deference, perhaps now under *Skidmore*, on judicial review.

- For issues regarding agency authority to make policy through adjudication, stress that this is a long-standing practice among agencies and is traditionally part of the common-law adjudicatory process. If *NLRB v. Wyman-Gordon Co.*, 394 U.S. 759 (1969), is relevant, state the views of both opinions in favor of the judgment since no view captured a majority.

Rulemaking exceptions

- If an agency makes a rule without notice and comment, look at the exceptions listed in APA §553 and go down the list to see if the agency's action falls within one of them.
    - Discuss the question in light of the definition of a legislative rule. Be sure to point out that legislative rules create binding law whereas nonlegislative rules do not.

Agency decisions without a formal process

- If an agency makes a decision with no formal process, look to the governing statute to see whether the agency was supposed to use an adjudicatory or legislative process. Also, be sure to point out any agency rules that require procedures in addition to those provided.
    - If no such requirement appears to exist, mention the APA requirement of providing an answer and a statement of reasons. Also, point out that if an agency does not use a formal process, any norm created cannot be considered binding law.

Exam Tips on APA RULEMAKING PROCEDURES

APA and rulemaking

- The starting place for all discussions of rulemaking procedure should be the APA.
    - For example, if you are asked a notice question, start with the language of §553's notice requirement and then move on to the major cases construing that requirement.

Bias and ex parte contacts

- In controversies regarding bias and ex parte contacts, it is useful to point out that the APA does not address these issues in informal rulemaking. Compare and contrast the various courts' approaches to the issues and then return to the APA and discuss whether one approach is more faithful to the APA.

Rulemaking procedures

- When answering questions regarding potential procedural defects in a rulemaking, in addition to the APA, support your analysis with the policies underlying the rulemaking process.
  - For example, in notice controversies, discuss whether the purpose of notice—providing fair notice so that interested parties may participate—is met or not.
  - In controversies regarding ex parte contacts and biased decision-makers, in addition to discussing the adequacy of the opportunity to participate, discuss the tension between rulemaking on a legal model and rulemaking as part of a political, legislative process.

Vermont Yankee

- If a party claims that an agency should have used more than §553 procedures in a rulemaking, look to see whether any statute or rule required more. If not, *Vermont Yankee* counsels against requiring more than §553.
- *Vermont Yankee* can be raised in all questions regarding procedural issues in rulemaking.
  - *Vermont Yankee*'s policies of predictability and procedural flexibility are implicated whenever a court is asked to read a provision of §553 broadly. It is thus effective to use *Vermont Yankee* as an argument against any but the most literal reading of the language of §553.
  - If the question raises an issue regarding whether an agency conducting informal rulemaking might be required to go beyond the procedures specified in §553, *Vermont Yankee* must be addressed.

Formal rulemaking

- In a question regarding whether an agency is required to use formal rulemaking procedures, it is important to note that the Supreme Court favors the more streamlined informal rulemaking process.
  - Be sure to point to the language of §553 and the particular agency's statute, and argue that unless the statute clearly requires a hearing and an "on the record" decision, formal rulemaking is not required.

Exam Tips on AGENCY ADJUDICATION AND DUE PROCESS

Public rights vs. private rights

- In any problem regarding the constitutionality of administrative adjudication, watch for the private rights issue.

- ☞ Pay attention to whether the right being adjudicated is within the core of Article III, or whether it is arguable that the adjudication at issue is in a category normally thought to be appropriate for a non-Article III tribunal.
- ☞ It also may be helpful to contrast Justice Brennan's categorical approach with the majority approach under which a much looser separation of powers standard applies.
- ☞ If the claim involves a civil penalty or any claim that resembles a traditional common-law claim, it would be helpful to argue that the subject of enforcement may be entitled to a jury trial in an Article III tribunal.

Property and liberty interests

- ☛ In due process cases, it is important to address first whether there is a protected interest, usually either property or liberty.
  - ☞ If the question involves property, clearly identify the source of any protected entitlement. Be creative and go beyond the bare words of state law when there is an argument for an implicit interest under *Perry v. Sindermann*, 408 U.S. 593 (1972).
  - ☞ In liberty cases, distinguish between "entitlement liberty" and "constitutional liberty."
  - ☞ In a constitutional liberty case, identify the nature of the protected liberty interest.
  - ☞ In an entitlement liberty case, identify the source and nature of the protected liberty interest.

What process is due?

- ☛ When deciding what process is due, analyze each element of the *Mathews v. Eldridge* test separately.
  - ☞ When applying the third element, look for indications that less procedure is desirable for reasons other than the state's pure desire to save time and resources on procedure (e.g., perhaps because an emergency necessitates quick action).
  - ☞ In employment cases, note that the Supreme Court has decided categorically that due process requires at least an informal pre-termination oral hearing.
  - ☞ In other areas, note that the Court has allowed for paper procedures pre-termination except when subsistence benefits are concerned, as in *Goldberg v. Kelly*, 397 U.S. 254 (1970).
  - ☞ Be sure to note that in most situations when a pre-termination oral hearing is not required, such a hearing must be provided post-termination.

Bias vs. prejudgment

- ☛ Be clear about the difference between bias and prejudgment, and discuss explicitly the facts that lead to an argument that one or the other is present.

Statutory right to a hearing

- In cases involving the statutory right to a hearing, identify the source of the right to a hearing. Look explicitly into whether statutes or regulations limit the scope of the hearing.
  - If there is a due process issue regarding a substantive limitation on the scope of a hearing, the irrebuttable presumption doctrine may be relevant in reinforcing the general rule that the scope of the hearing is tailored to the substantive issues as specified in the statute and regulations. However, it is important to note that the irrebuttable presumption doctrine is no longer good law.

Exam Tips on *SUBSTANTIVE POLICYMAKING IN AGENCIES*

- The material in this chapter can be used to supplement exam discussion of substantive standards on judicial review.
  - For example, on questions regarding substantive standards of review, discussion of reasoned decision-making and clarity and consistency requirements could supplement discussion of APA §706's arbitrary and capricious or substantial evidence standards of review.

Cost-benefit analysis

- In questions raising issues regarding cost-benefit analysis, the starting point should be the agency's statute—does it clearly require cost-benefit analysis? If not, then cost-benefit analysis is probably not required, although more recent cases may go the other way on this point.
  - A discussion of the strengths and weaknesses of cost-benefit analysis could supplement an answer raising cost-benefit issues.
- If an exam has a question in which an agency conducts a cost-benefit analysis, it might be useful to look at the agency's statute to determine whether the agency is allowed to do cost-benefit analysis or whether a statutory provision precludes it.

National Environmental Policy Act

- The most likely questions regarding NEPA concern the contents of the EIS and what the agency must do with the EIS once it is prepared.
  - In the latter regard, it may be helpful to explain the value of a purely procedural NEPA.
  - Be sure also to explain your answer in light of the text of NEPA, which provides only that the EIS must be prepared and must "accompany" the agency's proposal through all review stages.

Post-decision support

- Watch for agency arguments in support of agency action on grounds that were not relied on at the agency level, and point out that agency action must stand or fall on the grounds the agency relied on when it made its decision.

Clarity requirements

- In a question that raises clarity concerns, point out that the cases imposing clarity requirements on due process grounds may be out of date or inconsistent with the *Roth* line of cases regarding property interests.
  - Further, it is unclear whether, as a nonconstitutional matter, the APA imposes a similar requirement on federal agencies. It can be argued, however, that absent a clear standard, agency action is arbitrary.

Estoppel and nonacquiescence

- In a question raising the issue of whether the representations of an official can estop the agency, state the general rule that agencies are not estopped by such conduct. Point out that for constitutional reasons, the rule is even stronger when expenditure of funds is involved.
- In a question raising issues of collateral estoppel and agency nonacquiescence, it may be useful to explain why agencies may wish to adhere to their views without necessarily appealing every adverse ruling.
  - It is clear that nonmutual collateral estoppel does not apply against the government in litigation.
  - However, within a circuit that has rejected the agency's view, the rule of law may require the agency to acquiesce to the court's ruling.

Exam Tips on AGENCY ENFORCEMENT AND LICENSING

Prosecutorial discretion

- In questions about prosecutorial discretion, reviewability issues are likely to be very important.
  - Argue that exercises of prosecutorial discretion are presumptively unreviewable.
  - Then look for any indication that the agency's statute restricts or compels prosecutions under certain circumstances to rebut the presumption of unreviewability.

Discriminatory enforcement

- In questions raising claims of discriminatory enforcement, apply the "patent abuse of discretion" standard to claims of discriminatory enforcement, and discuss how difficult courts have made it to prevail on such claims.

Occupational and business licensing

- Occupational and business licensing exam questions are most likely to raise due process property interest questions.
  - Analyze the particular scheme under *Board of Regents v. Roth*, 408 U.S. 564 (1972), and then look for special problems such as capture of the licensing body by a segment of the profession or industry looking to avoid competition from another segment.
  - If capture appears to be present, discuss whether *Gibson v. Berryhill*, 411 U.S. 564 (1973), or *Friedman v. Rogers*, 440 U.S. 1 (1979), should govern. Recall that under *Friedman v. Rogers*, the *Gibson* rule may not extend beyond the context of disciplinary hearings. However, it may be worthwhile to raise antitrust concerns along with due process issues if an agency is dominated by a segment of a profession.

FCC licensing

- In FCC licensing questions, watch for questions raising *Ashbacker* and *Storer* issues.
  - On *Storer* issues, watch for an argument by the applicant that the FCC's rule should not apply in the particular case.
  - Note that comparative hearings are now required only on initial licensing decisions and not on renewals.

Ratemaking

- Ratemaking is not a common area for examination, except perhaps as an example of important issues that apply across the administrative law spectrum.
  - Due process hearing issues are important, since ratemaking is often conducted in a formal hearing.
  - In ratemaking questions, watch for *Morgan* issues, in which the decision-maker does not actually hear the evidence before deciding on the proper rate structure. If *Morgan* is relevant, point out that the later *Morgan* decisions make it difficult to police agency conduct in presiding over ratemaking proceedings. *See Morgan v. United States*, 298 U.S. 468 (1936), and *United States v. Morgan*, 313 U.S. 409 (1941).

Exam Tips on AGENCY INFORMATION GATHERING

- The most likely candidates for examination from the material in this chapter include warrantless inspections and the requirements for obtaining warrants, and the collective-entity rule regarding Fifth Amendment rights against self-incrimination.

Inspection

- In a question raising an issue regarding an inspection, discuss first any doubts that the agency has the authority to conduct inspections.
  - Then look to whether the agency had a warrant.
  - If the agency had a warrant, the warrant may be subject to attack if the inspection was not part of the routine operation of a regulatory scheme.
  - If the agency did not have a warrant, look to whether the search meets the requirements for warrantless searches of pervasively regulated businesses.

Drug testing

- In a question about drug testing, discuss whether the particular employee or employees that the government wants to test are in sensitive positions or have been involved in an incident justifying special scrutiny. Otherwise, the testing might not be proper.

Subpoena enforcement

- In a case involving production of documents or provision of information to the government, if it is relevant, raise the collective-entity rule and the rule that custodians of entity records may not raise Fifth Amendment objections to providing such records.
  - It also is useful to note that courts do not like issues of agency authority to be litigated in the context of the enforcement of a subpoena.
  - Finally, if a privilege such as the attorney-client privilege is raised, be sure to note that the applicability of state-law privileges to federal administrative proceedings has not been established.

Exam Tips on PRIVATE ENFORCEMENT OF REGULATORY NORMS AND PREEMPTION

- Except for preemption, the material in this chapter is rarely tested on because it is not central to most administrative law courses. The material on private rights of action and preemption may be tested on more often than the remainder of the material other than preemption.

Citizens' suits

- In any question regarding citizens' suits, the language of the particular citizens' suit provision should be the starting place for analysis.

- In a question regarding the relationship between citizens' suit provisions and judicial review, the *Bennett v. Spear*, 520 U.S. 154 (1997) provides the framework for understanding.
  - The important point is that citizens' suit provisions are narrow, allowing claims against the government only when the government fails to perform a nondiscretionary duty or violates the relevant statute as a regulated private party might violate it.
- Citizens' suits often raise standing issues.
  - You should distinguish between prudential limits on standing, such as the zone of interests test, which citizens' suit provision can affect, and constitutional standing requirements, which citizens' suit provisions cannot affect.

Implied private rights of action

- In a question about implied private rights of action, it may be useful to compare the current "intent of Congress" standard to the two standards that preceded it, the *J.I. Case* "advance the statutory purposes" standard, and the four-factor test of *Cort v. Ash*. *See J.I. Case v. Borak*, 377 U.S. 426 (1964), and *Cort v. Ash*, 422 U.S. 66 (1975).

Preemption

- In preemption questions, the starting point for analysis should be statutory language, including express preemption provisions, partial preemption provisions, and savings clauses.
  - If there is no express preemption provision, look for implied preemption through "field preemption," "actual conflict preemption," or "obstacle to the legislative purpose" preemption.

Judicial remedies and agency jurisdiction

- In a case involving overlap between judicial remedies and the jurisdiction of a federal agency, apply the primary jurisdiction doctrine.
  - If it appears that the agency has jurisdiction over a dispute, and the dispute is within the expertise of the agency, then there is an argument that a judicial remedy should not be allowed until the agency has had the opportunity to address the case.

Exam Tips on
LIABILITY OF AGENCIES AND OFFICIALS

- The issues in this chapter are not often tested on, since they are not at the core of administrative law. However, FTCA issues are sometimes tested on, and some instructors may include minor issues on the liability matters addressed herein.

Federal Tort Claims Act

- In answering any FTCA question, look carefully at the Act and ask whether a statutory basis for liability exists, and if so, whether an exception bars liability.
- In discussing the discretionary-function exception, which is the FTCA issue most likely to be tested, it may be helpful to discuss the regulatory functions exception that the Court rejected.
  - Be sure to spell out the governing test for the exception ("choice or judgment" and "the exercise of discretion in furtherance of public policy goals"), and compare the official activity in the examination with the official activity in cases such as *Gaubert v. United States*, 499 U.S. 315 (1991), and *Berkovitz v. United States*, 486 U.S. 531 (1988).

Liability of officials

- In a damages action against a government official, if the claim is a constitutional claim, the issue is whether a *Bivens* action is available.
  - Regarding *Bivens* actions, look for remedies that Congress has declared as substitutes for *Bivens* or for special factors counseling hesitation.
  - Be aware that even if Congress has not specified that an alternate remedy is a substitute for *Bivens*, it may displace the *Bivens* remedy as a special factor.
- With regard to official immunity from damages under either *Bivens* or §1983, apply the functional approach to determine whether the official should receive absolute immunity.
  - For officials entitled only to qualified immunity, remember that the subjective factor is no longer relevant, so that the official is liable only if he or she violated clearly established law.

Municipal liability

- With regard to municipal liability, watch for attempts to hold cities liable that are actually attempts to get around the ban on vicarious liability through some clever way of alleging a municipal policy or custom.
  - The Court is very strict on requiring a municipal policy, and it thus does not make it easy to hold cities liable for constitutional violations committed by city employees.
  - Thus, while claims for inadequate training or screening of employees exist in theory, you should be clear that such claims are very difficult to win because they are too close to vicarious liability.

Exam Tips on *FREEDOM OF INFORMATION AND OPEN MEETINGS*

- The most likely area in this chapter to be tested on is FOIA.
  - Likely questions include those asking about the coverage of FOIA (what are agency records?) and about FOIA exceptions.
- The other candidate for examination is the Government in the Sunshine Act, with questions focusing on what constitutes a meeting of an agency and whether an exception to the Sunshine Act allows for a private meeting.

Standing

- Standing questions also might come up in terms of who has standing to raise a FOIA or Sunshine Act issue in litigation, and who has standing to try to prevent an agency from disclosing information in response to a FOIA request.

Freedom of Information Act

- In a question about FOIA, be sure to cite and quote from the statutory provision at issue.
  - Be prepared to discuss whether particular information is contained in agency records.
  - Watch out for records that were not created by the agency or are not in the agency's possession and were not in the agency's possession at the time of the FOIA request.
- Regarding FOIA exceptions, be sure to quote the statutory provision and keep in mind that courts construe the exceptions narrowly.
  - Keep in mind that more than one exception may arguably apply to a particular agency record, and be sure to discuss all exceptions that might apply.
- In a case in which a party supplying information to the agency seeks to prevent the agency from providing records in response to a third party's FOIA request, discuss the issue in terms of the requirements for "reverse FOIA" actions.
  - Point out that the APA provides judicial review of an agency decision to release information, and that other statutes, such as the Trade Secrets Act and the Privacy Act, may provide a legal basis for reversing the agency on judicial review.
- Privacy-based FOIA exceptions are likely to be asked about. Be sure to discuss the balancing test used to determine whether the public's need to know is outweighed by a potential invasion of privacy.

Discovery against the government

- On any question regarding discovery from the government in litigation, be sure to point out that the government may resist discovery on all the grounds that other parties may employ and may raise evidentiary privileges and executive immunity.
  - In either case, the procedure for raising the objection, including whether the material is presumed to be available in discovery or presumed to be confidential, may be relevant.

Sunshine Act

- In questions about the Sunshine Act, be sure to consider whether an agency meeting is involved and whether the particular agency is covered by the Act.
  - If an agency meeting is involved, and an agency wishes to hold it in private, look at both the substance of the Sunshine Act's exceptions and whether the agency has followed proper procedures for closing a meeting.

ESSAY EXAM QUESTIONS AND ANSWERS

ESSAY EXAM QUESTIONS

QUESTION 1

The North American Free Trade Agreement (NAFTA) among Canada, the United States, and Mexico requires all three countries to admit each other's trucks for delivery of goods. However, the agreement does not prevent each country from enforcing environmental and safety rules. Because of this, trucks from Mexico have never been allowed to cross the border into the United States. Recently, an international tribunal established under NAFTA has ruled that the United States' ban on Mexican trucks violates NAFTA because it is not adequately justified on either environmental or safety grounds. The tribunal ordered the United States to reconsider whether to admit Mexican trucks. Under U.S. law, the responsibility for determining whether to admit foreign trucks to U.S. highways lies with the Department of Transportation. A statute directs the Secretary of Transportation to admit foreign trucks under the following legal requirements contained in the Foreign Transportation Act:

> Trucks from a foreign country "shall be admitted to the United States if either (a) the Secretary concludes and certifies that the nation in which the trucks are registered imposes environmental and safety requirements that are as stringent or more stringent than those in force in the United States or (b) the Secretary concludes and certifies that admittance of the trucks from the foreign nation will not result in significant impairment to the clean air interests of the United States or impose significant safety risks within the United States. In making the foregoing determinations, the Secretary shall conduct a full environmental review whenever a preliminary review indicates that it is clear that significant environmental harm is likely."

President George W. Bush is eager to comply with the tribunal's ruling and issues the following directive to the Department of Transportation: "I hereby direct that the Secretary of Transportation shall conduct an expedited review of the eligibility of trucks from the nation of Mexico to travel within the United States and that a full environmental impact review shall be conducted only if, after a preliminary review, it is clear that significant environmental harm is likely if Mexican trucks are admitted to travel within the United States." President Bush also persuades his Mexican counterpart to adopt safety regulations identical to those for trucks in the United States.

This directive is immediately challenged in federal court by the Teamsters Union, which represents a large percentage of truck drivers in the United States. A significant number of the Union's members work for companies that transfer Mexican goods to U.S. trucks at the border for transportation into the United States. They allege that the National Environmental Policy Act requires a full environmental review and that the President's directive improperly pressures the Secretary of Transportation to admit Mexican trucks to the United States.

Part A. You are clerking for the federal district judge to whom this case has been assigned. The judge wants a memo on whether this directive is subject to immediate judicial review in a petition brought by the Teamsters Union. Please write the memo.

Assume that the first challenge was denied and the Secretary of Transportation's review goes forward. The Teamsters Union submits comments based on studies by reputable scientists showing that the admittance of Mexican trucks will result in an additional 100 highway deaths per year. Eighty percent of these deaths will be caused by increased traffic on the roads in the Southwest United States including California, but 20 percent will be caused by mechanical failures due to lax safety inspections in Mexico, which, according to the Teamsters, amounts to noncompliance with the Foreign Transportation Act's safety provision. (Traffic will increase because currently loads are usually consolidated when goods are transferred to U.S. trucks at the border; without the need to transfer, the Teamsters' studies predict that this consolidation will not occur.) The comments also show that the number of days with unclean air in the Southwest will increase by approximately ten per year, partly because of increased traffic but mostly because of the fact that the Mexican trucks will emit more pollution than their American counterparts. The Teamsters' studies and comments conclude that this increase in pollution is significant and will result in unclean air and increases in respiratory illnesses and discomfort among residents in the Southwest, including Teamsters and their families, mainly in border areas with the highest concentration of Mexican trucks. The Teamsters' comments include statements from members residing in the border areas with respiratory illnesses that are aggravated by diesel pollution and who limit their own and their children's outdoor activities on days when unclean air is reported.

The Department of Transportation's own studies, also conducted by reputable scientists, show a lower number of predicted highway deaths and less pollution. A number of factors contribute to the Department's conclusions. For one, the Department concludes that for economic reasons, Mexican trucking companies will continue to consolidate their loads at the border, although now the consolidation will occur in Mexican trucks. The Department also concludes that Mexico's adoption of U.S. safety standards satisfies the Foreign Transportation Act's safety requirement, and the Department assumes that all of Mexico's safety requirements will be enforced. The Department of Transportation's study also concludes that the increased pollution from Mexican trucks is de minimis when considered in light of all the truck pollution in the United States, adding less than 0.01 percent to the diesel pollution from all sources. Based on the conclusion that neither safety nor pollution problems will significantly increase, the Secretary of Transportation decides to allow the Mexican trucks into the United States without conducting a full-scale environmental review. All of these conclusions, including the Secretary's disagreements with the conclusions of the Teamsters' studies, are included in a formally sufficient, concise general statement published together with the Secretary's decision.

Part B. The judge you are clerking for wants to know whether the Secretary's decision is now subject to judicial review, whether the Teamsters Union is the proper party to seek review, and what the outcome of judicial review should be, assuming it is available. Please write a memo to the judge addressing these issues. Do not worry about NEPA — assume that compliance with the Foreign Transportation Act would satisfy NEPA. You may refer to your analysis in Part A without repeating it.

SAMPLE ANSWER TO QUESTION 1 (BASED ON A STUDENT ANSWER)

Part A. The first issue is whether the Union has standing to challenge the directive. In general, the Union might have standing on behalf of its members if they were going to lose jobs or pay as a result of reduced working hours, and it might have standing on its own behalf due to lost dues from workers who lose jobs and leave the Union. To have standing on behalf of its members, the Union would have to meet the requirements of associational standing. Associational standing has three requirements: (1) there must be members who have standing, (2) the issue must be germane to the purposes of the association, and (3) the absence of the members must not present a problem in the litigation. The Union easily meets the second and third requirements—safeguarding jobs is easily germane to the purposes of a labor union, and given that it is seeking injunctive relief that is common to all members, there is no problem if the individuals do not sue. The first requirement, that members have standing, is problematic.

Article III standing requires that the plaintiff be injured, that the injury be caused by the challenged conduct, and that the injury be redressable—that is, the court could order a remedy that would rectify the injury. Here, there is probably no standing for several related reasons. First, it does not appear that anyone has been injured by the directive. Second, even if the Secretary ultimately allows the trucks in the country, causation is not clear for the simple reason that it is not clear that the Secretary will do anything in reaction to the directive that the Secretary would not have done without the directive. The directive looks as though it merely repeats what the statute says. It's almost as if the President wanted to make some political points but realized that he could not order the Secretary to act contrary to the statute, so he just repeated the statute. The only thing the President added is that the preliminary review be "expedited." This seems within the President's power as head of the executive branch—"expedited" does not mean "deficient." There is no suggestion that the President is exerting undue influence by raising issues not related to the merits, and there is nothing secret or ex parte here. The standing problem also bleeds into ripeness—unless and until the Secretary takes action, it is unclear whether anyone will be hurt by the directive.

An additional standing problem is the zone of interests test. Workers may not be in the zone of interests of the law regulating foreign trucks. The law seems to be concerned primarily with highway safety and air pollution, not with jobs for American workers. The workers are like the postal workers in the case in which the Supreme Court found that labor unions were not in the zone of interests of the law regulating the postal service's monopoly. However, in this case, given the intense political discussions surrounding NAFTA, it may be that workers' interests were considered in Congress's consideration of the Act. If so, then the workers and their Union would be within the zone of interests.

There are some arguments that point in favor of standing at this time. First, like the *General Contractors'* case and *Bennett v. Spear*, it's not the final outcome that the Union is challenging; it's the process that seemed rigged against its members' interests. The injury is not the ultimate decision, but it forces them to participate in a process that will not adequately consider their interests. This is a weak argument because the process is not obviously rigged the way that minority set-aside laws require decisions based on race. Second, the Union can argue for a procedural injury. Even Justice Scalia has said that a person affected by an agency action can challenge the procedures used even when the person cannot prove that the decision would have been different had proper procedure been followed. The problem here, which bleeds into the merits of the case, is that the directive does not order the Secretary to change the procedures except that the preliminary review be "expedited." All "expedited" means is "do it now" and maybe "faster than normal." Nothing indicates that the review would violate any statute, so it's really unclear what problem the Union has.

There are also significant finality and ripeness problems with bringing a challenge to the directive before the Secretary has acted. Until the Secretary decides whether to allow in the trucks, there is no final agency action allowing judicial review under the APA. The President's directive is not final agency action for two reasons: first, because the President is not an agency and, second, because the directive merely structures the procedure for the future; it does not decide whether to actually do anything. Even if there were final agency action, a challenge might not be ripe. Because we don't know what the Secretary is actually going to do, a challenge to the directive might not be fit, and there might not be hardship in delaying review. It's not fit because we don't know what the Secretary is actually going to do—will he rush the review and approve the trucks without adequate consideration of environmental factors? There is no hardship because no one is going to lose any jobs unless and until the Secretary decides to allow in the trucks, and nothing will prevent the Union from seeking review then. It seems like finality and ripeness will be met only when the Secretary makes a final decision on whether to admit the trucks.

Part B. Now that the Secretary has allowed the trucks into the United States, the Union's challenge to that decision is ripe, and the Secretary's decision is final for the purposes of the APA. The Union would still have to overcome the associational standing hurdle, but assuming that one member will have reduced hours or lose a job, there should be sufficient injury to allow standing even to challenge the decision not to conduct a full environmental review. This would be allowed based on procedural injury to someone who is genuinely injured by the agency's decision. Further, it may be enough for standing that U.S. truckers will now face competition from foreign truckers.

One issue may be jurisdiction, although we don't have sufficient information to resolve it. If any statute points toward review of final orders of the Secretary in the Court of Appeals, the District Court should order the case transferred to that court. In general, for reasons of judicial economy, the courts prefer for review to start in the Court of Appeals whenever statutes allow. We would have to look at the statutes governing judicial review of Department of Transportation decisions to resolve this issue.

On the substance, the first question is whether the Secretary's conclusion that a full environmental review was unnecessary was arbitrary and capricious. The arbitrary, capricious test applies because this was an informal decision—there is no indication that the procedures were on the record with a hearing that would trigger substantial evidence review. The arbitrary, capricious test may have been satisfied by the Secretary's apparent consideration of the evidence on both sides and the fact that both sides had reputable scientific evidence. If the Secretary took a hard look at the evidence on both sides, and if the Secretary applied the correct legal standard, that would be sufficient. One complication was whether the way the Secretary dismissed the pollution as adding little to the nation's overall pollution was unreasonable. Can the health effects on local residents be dismissed as insignificant in light of the nation's overall pollution, which won't be increased very much? This is a tough one to answer and might require consideration of the legislative intent behind the Act. Overall, however, because some of the issues—for example, on consolidation and safety—are matters within the Secretary's expertise, review should be deferential.

The Union may argue that the Secretary misconstrued the authority to proceed without a full environmental review and also misconstrued the substantive requirements of the Act relating to clean air and safety. The Union may argue that the Secretary's own conclusions on the environment and safety reveal that there will be *significant* environmental problems and *significant* safety risks, and thus the statute prohibits the approval and requires a full environmental review. Before it was overruled, this may have raised a *Chevron* issue: Did Congress directly speak to the precise question at issue, and, if not, was the Secretary's construction permissible? If *Chevron* applied, the agency would probably prevail. The word "significant" is ambiguous enough to get to step two on all issues: the approval and the decision to proceed without a full environmental review. And the Secretary's understanding seems within the realm of reason under step two, given how deferential step two was. But now, with *Chevron* overruled and *Loper Bright* instructing courts to arrive at the best reading of the statute, review of agency statutory interpretation should be more straightforward. However, in *Loper Bright*, the Court also raised the possibility that courts might defer under *Skidmore* to well-considered long-standing agency statutory constructions. Regardless, it seems that the Secretary is following the plain text of the statute and thus deference may be irrelevant. The agency is simply correct on the statute's meaning.

Another issue is whether the decision should be overturned because of excessive influence by the President, via the directive. Here, as discussed above, the directive should not be a problem. The President did not ask the Secretary to violate the statute, only to follow it quickly. It was done aboveboard and out in the open, and matters extraneous to the issues at hand were not raised. It may be that the Secretary decided out of loyalty to the President, but that could be viewed as a good thing given the President's political accountability, and as long as the record supports the decision, there is no legal problem.

There is a slight hint of unreviewability because the Act seems to place things in the discretion of the Secretary. However, the language is insufficient to support a conclusion that the decision is "committed to agency discretion by law." There are certainly clear legal standards to apply, and the statute does not make the Secretary's decision subjective or indicate that there should be no review.

In conclusion, although the decision to allow the Mexican trucks in the United States is final and ripe, and the plaintiff has standing, the decision probably survives review under the applicable standard of review.

QUESTION 2

(Note: The statutes discussed may have been modified for this problem.) The federal Food, Drug and Cosmetic Act prohibits the use of any "drug" as a food additive without the specific approval of the FDA. The Act contains no definition of a "drug."

The FDA is an agency within the Department of Health and Human Services, which is headed by a single commissioner. The Commissioner has the full power to act on behalf of the agency, including issuing policy statements, regulations (and other such things), and the power to review adjudications conducted under the Act. The Act grants the FDA the power to issue "such rules and regulations necessary to carry out the provisions of the Act." The Act also authorizes the FDA to hold hearings on alleged violations and issue fines and cease-and-desist orders against violations. The Act provides that the initial hearing is held before an administrative law judge "not under the supervision, direct or indirect, of any employee of the Food and Drug Administration." Appeal is to the Commissioner, who has all the power of the initial decision-maker, with substantial evidence judicial review "in the court of appeals for the circuit in which the party charged has its main place of business or in which the violation is alleged to have taken place, at the option of the party seeking review."

Since the passage of the Act, the FDA has interpreted the Act not to cover chemicals found naturally in any food product. Thus it has not regulated the use of caffeine in soft drinks, since caffeine occurs naturally in coffee and chocolate. A 1965 policy statement (issued by its then-commissioner) stated that "[i]t is the policy of the FDA not to require approval for any food additive found naturally in a commonly consumed food product as long as the concentrations of such additive are no greater than concentrations naturally occurring in other food products."

The debate over whether cigarettes should be regulated because of evidence that cigarette manufacturers were carefully setting the amount of nicotine in cigarettes sparked interest in whether soft drink manufacturers were engaged in similar manipulation of the amount of caffeine in soft drinks. Critics cited the advertising of Jolt Cola that "all the sugar and twice the caffeine" was evidence that soft drinks were being spiked with caffeine to maintain sales of soft drinks. Critics also cited evidence that some drinks, such as Mountain Dew and Mellow Yellow, contained as much caffeine per serving as coffee and that caffeine is mildly addictive because halting caffeine use can cause headaches and other physical symptoms.

In early 1996, the FDA issued a policy statement providing: "The FDA will now apply the Food, Drug and Cosmetic Act to require approval as additives for all drugs used as food additives, including those that are found naturally in a commonly consumed food product, even if the concentrations of such additives are no greater than concentrations naturally occurring in other food products. Because this is not a legislative rule, section 553 procedural requirements do not apply." The FDA then conducted research on caffeine in soft drinks. Immediately after the issuance of the 1996 FDA statement, several soft drink manufacturers removed caffeine from their products.

Needless to say, soft drink manufacturers and the manufacturers of caffeine additive powder were not happy with this turn of events. They are seeking advice on what steps they might be able to take now to prevent the FDA from going forward with its research. They also wonder whether any other of the FDA's actions thus far violate the APA and can be challenged at this time. You have been hired by the soft drink manufacturers and the caffeine additive manufacturers to provide legal advice on what steps they might take at this point. Early in your research, you discover from a disgruntled FDA employee that before the 1996 statement was issued, the Commissioner of the FDA had extensive contacts regarding the effects of caffeine with health-care advocates, and at a private research session, he was shown a great deal of evidence regarding the negative effects of caffeine and the prevalence of caffeine addiction among children who drink Mountain Dew and eat chocolate. Also, the FDA Commissioner generally refused to meet with soft drink and caffeine industry lobbyists, citing potential conflicts of interest.

Part A. Please write a memorandum regarding potential challenges at this stage and any issues that might be available on judicial review at a later stage.

(New facts below for Part B)

Assume that the FDA's research continued and ultimately the FDA enforcement bureau brought an enforcement complaint against Jake Cola, Inc., a small Los Angeles-based manufacturer of high-priced organic cola drinks. Jake Cola contains far less caffeine than the leading brands of cola drinks such as Coca-Cola and Pepsi-Cola. Jake Cola's market share is minuscule; it has approximately less than 0.1 percent of the market share in the Los Angeles area and only $50,000 worth of business outside California, annually. (Assume that this is sufficient to meet any "interstate commerce" requirements for federal regulation.) In fact, Jake Cola advertises that it has less caffeine than the other brands and shows on its label the actual number of milligrams of caffeine per serving, which no other brand does.

In an informal conversation, Jake's lawyer asked the FDA prosecutor why Jake Cola was being singled out at this time. The FDA prosecutor responded that the FDA has an informal policy of prosecuting companies that advertise regarding the additive at issue, and also the FDA usually goes after small companies first to establish a principle that can be applied in later cases against larger companies that, in the words of the prosecutor, "might put up more of a defense." Jake Cola's lawyer then asked whether an enforcement action was being brought against Jolt, which advertises "twice the caffeine." The FDA prosecutor said no and also said he thinks it is related to the fact that Jolt has a lobbyist who used to be general counsel at the FDA.

Part B. Jake Cola's lawyer heard from Jake's caffeine supplier about your earlier work regarding this matter and would like to know whether any of this additional information might either help Jake Cola prevent the hearing from occurring or supply grounds for reversing any adverse decision later on judicial review. Do not address any potential First Amendment issues.

(New facts below for Part C)

Assume that the hearing against Jake Cola went forward. The ALJ, although finding a violation of the Act, since Jake Cola admittedly adds caffeine without FDA approval, declined to issue a cease-and-desist order or impose a fine on the grounds that "Jake Cola is a small player in the soft drink market and uses less caffeine than most. An order should not issue unless other, larger soft drink manufacturers are also prosecuted." The FDA prosecutor then sought review before the Commissioner. The Commissioner, after reviewing the record of the ALJ hearing and receiving briefs from Jake and the prosecutor, found that Jake Cola was in violation of the Act, that a cease-and-desist order should issue, and that a fine was not proper at this time. The Commissioner, in the conclusion of his opinion, stated the following:

> I hereby find that caffeine is a drug and that as such it may not be added to food products without specific approval from the FDA. Accordingly, allowing for the sale of existing stocks, any manufacturer or distributor of a food product in violation of this ruling thirty days after the date of this order will be assessed substantial fines for violating the Act.

Part C. At this point, your original clients (soft drink manufacturers and makers of caffeine additives) seek your advice on whether they now have grounds to bring suit against the FDA. They would like your advice on whether there are any procedural or substantive grounds for challenging the Commissioner's apparent order that they stop the use of caffeine in soft drinks and other food products and whether the Commissioner can be prevented from participating in further proceedings on the issue. Please write a memorandum concerning these issues.

SAMPLE ANSWER TO QUESTION 2 (BASED ON A STUDENT ANSWER)

Part A. The first issue is whether there is a dispute that is ripe for review at this time. All the FDA has done is announce that it will take enforcement action in a category of cases in the future and has begun to conduct research to that end. It has not taken action against anyone yet. Assuming that judicial review is available for any enforcement order issued, there may not be any reason to allow judicial review at this time. Further, the statement may be unfit for review because it is not clear what the FDA will actually do under it. The FDA might be very strict and reject most applications, or it might be very liberal and grant most applications to use additives that occur naturally.

Assuming that review is available now, or perhaps later, there are several grounds for challenging the FDA's new policy. First, the manufacturers may argue that the policy statement is a legislative rule and should have been promulgated with a notice-and-comment process. This is not a very strong argument. The strongest argument for the challengers is that the FDA will act in the future as if it is bound to take action against caffeine and other similar additives. The new interpretation of the Act also adds to the law since the FDA claims the power to take enforcement action that it previously said it could not take. However, despite these arguments, when an agency announces its enforcement policy, it is considered a policy statement, and the agency does not have to use a notice-and-comment process. Further, this particular statement is arguably interpretive, since it construes the word "drug" and the terms of the agency's power to regulate food additives. A court on judicial review after an enforcement order might reject these interpretations, and the agency's statement is not a binding legal obligation until an enforcement order is actually issued and upheld on judicial review.

Another issue is whether the FDA's view that caffeine is a drug is consistent with the statute. Here, by not defining "drug," Congress left a gap or created an ambiguity. Previously, the agency's interpretation may have received deference under *Chevron*, although perhaps not since it was an informally issued policy statement without notice and comment. However, now that *Chevron* is no longer good law, the courts would determine the meaning of the statute independently, with respect for the agency's determination under *Skidmore*. Because this is a new interpretation and is directly contrary to the agency's prior view, *Skidmore* would not require much, if any, deference to the agency's view. Without knowing more about the history of the statute, it is difficult to predict how a court would react to the agency's new interpretation. If the legislative history of the statute reveals that Congress would not have wanted the FDA to regulate caffeine, then perhaps a court would overrule the agency. There are good arguments on both sides of the statutory issue.

The next issue has to do with the extensive ex parte contacts that occurred prior to the issuance of the statement. Nothing in the APA prohibits these contacts except in formal proceedings. In fact, without any sort of notice-and-comment process, it is difficult to imagine any legal doctrine that would prevent the agency from having contacts with anyone it wants to. If there had been an actual rulemaking, then a court might have required the agency to place all the information it had on the record for comment. Insofar as the agency appears to be using the statement plus the threat of prosecution as a substitute for a rulemaking, some courts might be suspicious of what the agency did. However, it is unclear whether anything could be done at this point. The whole process seems unfair, but there is no apparent remedy.

In sum, it is unlikely that a court would prevent the agency from conducting research and from issuing a policy statement that informs the public that it intends to prosecute certain cases in the future. Perhaps a rule on prosecutions would be unreviewable as committed to agency discretion by law. In any case, judicial review is not likely to be available until the agency brings an enforcement proceeding or promulgates a legislative rule.

Part B. These facts raise a claim of discriminatory enforcement. Jake Cola would argue that it is a patent abuse of discretion for the FDA to prosecute when Jake Cola has less caffeine than most other sodas and when its market share, even in its local area, is minuscule. The agency would have to articulate some reason for its choice. Courts are so deferential to agency enforcement priorities that the agency might be upheld if it says something as empty as "We chose this company as one of many that we ultimately intend to prosecute." Further, putting First Amendment concerns aside, the agency might rely on a policy of prosecuting companies that mention caffeine, and it could say, "We are looking into whether we should bring an action against Jolt." On the one hand, if a court took the possibility of a discriminatory-enforcement claim seriously, this should be a good case. There is no question that the other sodas have caffeine—unlike in the *Universal-Rundle* case, in which the agency could say it was an open question whether the other companies were violating the law. On the other hand, it is not clear how badly Jake Cola would be hurt if it could not use caffeine. After all, it uses very little, and there are colas without caffeine on the market. And this is not a case in which the statute is concerned with preserving competition, which made the unsuccessful discriminatory enforcement claim in *Universal-Rundle* stronger than this one.

It should be noted that the discriminatory-enforcement issue may not be ripe for review until the agency actually issues an order against Jake Cola. There is no final order and no other obvious basis for immediate judicial review. There is neither fitness nor hardship. We don't really know what order, if any, will be issued; we also do not know what effect the order will have. The cost of defending is not sufficient hardship.

Part C. First, there is no problem with the agency reversing the ALJ since credibility is not an issue. The basis for the reversal is a matter of policy that the agency should be able to decide itself. The ALJ's discriminatory-enforcement decision is entitled to no deference from the agency. Although a court should take it into account on judicial review, it is purely an issue of policy, and the agency should be free to reverse it.

At this point, there is no ripeness problem since a final order has been issued. The discriminatory enforcement issue is ripe because a cease-and-desist order has been issued. The analysis in Part B should be applied to the claim.

There is also a question of standing. Do the other soft drink manufacturers or the caffeine producers have standing? It seems clear that the drink makers do have standing in that they are likely to be subjected to an order to change their product in the very near future. They are directly regulated, so the zone of interests is not an issue. The caffeine makers are injured directly by the agency action since the market for their product will shrink (and has already shrunk), but there is a zone of interests question, since nothing in the Act is concerned with the interests of ingredient makers. Further, they would be asserting the rights of third parties (the drink manufacturers) who are perfectly able to assert their own rights. Finally, their presence does not really add anything to the case. I would be inclined to allow them to have standing because it does not really hurt anything. They are clearly injured, but a strict court might deny them standing on the ground that they are asserting third-party rights and are not within the zone of interests of the law in question.

The main question here is whether it is proper for the Commissioner to include what looks like a rule about caffeine in his decision in the case about Jake Cola. He says he will seek large fines in the future even though he has not fined Jake at all. In the *Wyman-Gordon* case, some members of the Court thought this is fine, since prospective rules are part of the judicial process. Others think it is fine because future subjects will be fined only after a hearing. The dissenters thought that if an agency wants to make a general rule, it should have to use the rulemaking procedure of the APA. In my view, the Commissioner will be upheld. The rule announced here is about the particular additive caffeine. The FDA proceeds largely through enforcement actions. It seems appropriate, under *Bell Aerospace*, for it to decide case-by-case which additives will be treated as drugs. As long as future subjects are given hearings, I see nothing wrong with announcing a strong precedent in the course of an adjudication. Here, a retroactive rule would be worse than the prospective one, since the agency is at least warning people before it issues fines.

The question remains, however, whether the Commissioner can announce this rule in an opinion and then rely on it in later prosecutions for levying fines. Here, if the Commissioner does not explicitly state, "I am assessing a large fine because the Jake Cola rule has been violated," there is not much of a problem. The Commissioner should state that the fine is because of the violation found at the hearing and cite Jake Cola as a precedent. The Commissioner will probably argue that he did not issue any rule in Jake Cola; he just stated what he intended to do in future cases. Those cases would still be decided on their own merits, and the violation would be for putting a drug in food, not for violating any aspect of the Jake Cola opinion.

The clients might argue that the Commissioner is biased or has prejudged the law in these cases and should not be allowed to sit on review of ALJ decisions. This argument sounds good, but it would basically destroy the system Congress has established for agency review of ALJ decisions. Agencies often announce rules and then sit as a reviewing tribunal. The agency is no more biased than a court that has announced a precedent and then has a later case on the same issue. Prejudgment raises the same issue. The Commissioner made no statements indicating a view on any pending matter, so there isn't evidence to support the appearance of prejudgment. To win on this argument, there would have to be a showing that the Commissioner is simply unwilling to even look at the evidence in the case. This looks more like the standard for prejudgment in a rulemaking. In effect, on policy decisions, the Commissioner should be judged on the rulemaking standard to allow him to carry out the functions Congress has assigned. Just as some judges have clear views on issues, like the death penalty or separation of powers, the Commissioner is free to express those views in cases as long as in subsequent cases the Commissioner is willing to look at the evidence and weigh the arguments.

In sum, I do not see any basis for reversing the Commissioner or disqualifying him from hearing future cases.

QUESTION 3

Since 1933, prices paid by handlers of milk to producers of milk have been set by the Secretary of Agriculture under what are denominated as Marketing Orders. Handlers, in turn, sell milk to food producers for use in prepared foods and to local dairies for public sale in retail stores. The Secretary's authority to establish Marketing Orders derives from the Agricultural Marketing Agreement Act. A section of this statute provides:

> The price of milk paid by milk handlers to milk producers shall be set by the Secretary, in his discretion, after hearing, to reflect the price of feeds, the available supplies of feeds, and other economic conditions which affect market supply and demand for milk or its products in the marketing area to which the contemplated marketing agreement, order, or amendment relates. Whenever the Secretary in his discretion finds, upon the basis of the evidence adduced at the hearing required by this section that the price of milk is not reasonable in view of the price of feeds, the available supplies of feeds, and other economic conditions which affect market area supply and demand for milk in the marketing area, he shall fix such prices as he finds will reflect such factors, insure a sufficient quantity of pure and wholesome milk to meet current needs and further to assure a level of farm income adequate to maintain productive capacity sufficient to meet anticipated future needs, and be in the public interest. Thereafter, as the Secretary finds necessary on account of changed circumstances, he shall, after due notice and opportunity for hearing, make adjustments in such prices.

The reference to "marketing area" in this provision concerns the Secretary's statutory authority to divide the nation into regions and to issue different Marketing Orders for each. Under this authority the Secretary has delineated 40 marketing areas, and every time he has set a price that handlers must pay milk producers for milk to be sold in a marketing area east of the Rocky Mountains he has added a differential based on the distance of the center of the area from Eau Claire, Wisconsin, the hub of the nation's traditional milk-producing region. This differential was established after a notice-and-comment rulemaking in 1934. In this rulemaking the Secretary explained that he interpreted the phrase "other economic conditions" to include consideration of distance from the center of the nation's milk-producing region because places distant from this center were not receiving adequate supplies of milk. The Secretary stated that the distance-from-Eau Claire price differential would encourage the transportation of milk into all marketing areas. In 1935, a court of appeals held that the Secretary's rule was supported by substantial evidence and was not arbitrary and capricious.

Since the adoption of this pricing system, milk shortages have not occurred in any regions. During this period, milk production also has become more dispersed in the Eastern United States, a dispersal that perhaps has been encouraged by the higher prices that milk handlers must pay for milk which is to be sold in regions more distant from Eau Claire. Nonetheless, the Secretary has not adjusted the pricing system, except periodically, through notice-and-comment rulemaking, to adjust for changes in the differential due to inflation in shipping costs.

Last year, the Secretary issued a notice that he was considering a minor increase in milk prices to adjust for inflation. Consumer groups, milk handlers, dairy farmers in areas relatively close to Eau Claire, food producers in areas distant from Eau Claire, and retail grocery companies from around the country all commented that the entire system of setting milk prices is obsolete and that the reference to Eau Claire, Wisconsin, should be abandoned, because distance from this city has no relation to the actual cost of producing and supplying milk. Milk producers in areas distant from Eau Claire and others commented on other issues, but did not address the Eau Claire-based differential. Both camps of milk producers, however, heavily lobbied the Secretary and his assistants as well as members of Congress, expressing their contrasting views on the retention of the existing milk marketing order price structure.

The Secretary has now promulgated a regulation making the minor adjustments to milk prices he proposed last year. In an accompanying statement, the Secretary explained that the "existing pricing system is maintained with minor adjustments for inflation in shipping and other costs." The Secretary did not make findings on the specific economic factors listed in the statute and did not respond to the comments that argued that the traditional factors used in setting prices were obsolete.

Consumer groups, Wisconsin milk producers, and food producers in areas distant from Eau Claire would like to seek judicial review of the Secretary's failure to alter the system for setting milk prices. Analyze whether each of these groups has standing to seek such review. Then consider the merits of the arguments they might advance against the Secretary. Is the 1935 circuit court decision upholding the system relevant to any of these arguments? What other information would you like to have? (Ignore what you know about the actual regulation of milk pricing and the case on which this problem is based.)

SAMPLE ANSWER TO QUESTION 3 (BASED ON A MEMO TO STUDENTS AFTER THE EXAM)

First, the standing of each group of potential plaintiffs should be addressed. The basic requirements for standing should be laid out, including injury traceable to the challenged conduct and redressability. Consumer groups have standing if members pay more for milk than under an alternative regulatory scheme they claim should replace the current scheme for milk pricing. Although many people share in the injury, because the price-setting scheme probably increases the price of milk, consumer complaints should not fail based on the generalized grievance doctrine because the consumers of milk are suing over something that affects them directly based on particular market activity, not merely by virtue of being a member of society. There also should be a brief discussion of the requirements for associational standing. Wisconsin milk producers have standing because the system for setting milk prices affects them directly in that it prescribes the price they are paid for their product. Even if deregulation might ultimately hurt them if prices moved lower, they are now not able to compete for business based on price, and that restriction is enough of an injury for standing. Food producers in areas distant from Eau Claire are injured because they pay more for milk than producers closer to Eau Claire, which in turn hurts their ability to compete with food producers near Eau Claire. Thus, it appears that all the potential plaintiffs are injured sufficiently for standing.

On the merits, this question raises a very interesting issue: If an agency takes an action, and that action has been upheld on judicial review, can changed circumstances render that action arbitrary and capricious or lacking in substantial evidence so that a challenge years after the action was upheld on judicial review could prevail? It appears that the substantial evidence test might apply here if the Secretary held a formal hearing. If not, review could still be had under the arbitrary and capricious test. Since it is not clear whether there really is a difference between the two tests when reviewing policy decisions of the sort at issue here, the specific test will be mentioned only when it might make a difference.

One issue might be reviewability, since the statute says that the Secretary shall make changes "as the Secretary finds necessary." This looks like a deeming clause in that it appears to vest substantial discretion in the Secretary. However, this type of phrasing is not sufficient to overcome the presumption in favor of judicial review. From what the facts indicate, action under this program has been subjected to judicial review since at least 1935. The same phrase also says that under certain circumstances the Secretary "shall" make adjustments to milk prices, indicating a legally enforceable obligation to do so. Further, there is no basis for holding this as unreviewable prosecutorial discretion, since the statute states pretty clearly when the Secretary is required to act.

Turning to the merits, the challenge is really not to the failure to act for sixty years but to the latest action that the Secretary took (i.e., making only minor adjustments to milk prices when the comments urged the Secretary to make substantial changes based on changed circumstances, which is exactly what the statute appears to tell the Secretary to do). Here, the question is whether, based on everything in the record, a reasonable person could have reached this conclusion (substantial evidence), or whether the Secretary considered the relevant factors, applied the correct legal standard, and made a clear error in judgment (arbitrary and capricious). It would be useful to have more information about exactly what information the record contains. Further, there may be a procedural problem, since the Secretary did not address the major issue of the obsolescence of the pricing system in the concise general statement and did not make findings on the issues specified in the statute. While formal findings are not required, courts can insist on a reasoned explanation of major statutory and policy issues in the concise general statement without violating *Vermont Yankee*'s prohibition on additional procedural requirements.

The fact that a court, in 1935, upheld this pricing system does not answer whether it is error for the Secretary to issue an order maintaining the 1935 system in light of today's circumstances. While a court might be reluctant to hold that an agency must revise regulations periodically to adjust for changing conditions, here the statute itself, and thus Congress, requires revision, so the 1935 decision should not really matter.

The final issue is ex parte contacts. Although the facts are not very specific, it appears that there was a great deal of lobbying going on from both sides. Some courts have held that ex parte contacts should not occur. If this were a formal adjudicatory hearing or a formal rulemaking, the ex parte contacts would present a reason under the APA to send the matter back to the agency for a new decision. Ex parte contacts are forbidden in such proceedings. If this were informal rulemaking or informal adjudication, nothing in the APA prohibits ex parte contacts. Some courts have prohibited them, especially when the rulemaking resolves a competing claim to a valuable privilege, but this may violate *Vermont Yankee* by imposing a procedural requirement not contained in the APA. The court could say that it is merely enforcing §553 by giving everyone an equal, adequate opportunity to participate in the rulemaking, but it is unclear whether the Supreme Court would accept this. More in keeping with *Vermont Yankee*, agencies in informal rulemaking can probably receive ex parte contacts but should place any important information on the record. As long as there is no suggestion that ex parte contacts involved irrelevant factors such as funding of other agency projects and the like, a system that allows ex parte contacts in rulemaking is probably better than one that attempts to prohibit them.

As a last comment, it should be noted that the agency might have run into trouble had it decided in this proceeding to radically alter the milk pricing system. It is not altogether clear that the interests in favor of preserving the system were aware that this was a possibility raised by some of the comments. Perhaps they were, since they did support their interests in ex parte contacts. But the notice did not raise the possibility, and if an agency wants to make a substantial change to long-standing practice, it should probably provide better notice than it did in this case, so that any change will not materially alter the proposal or not be a logical outgrowth of the proposal. Otherwise, interested parties might not realize that they should comment to protect their interests.

QUESTION 4

(This question is fictional, and no environmental statutes not referred to in the question should be consulted.) The Environmental Protection Agency (EPA) is concerned about air pollution resulting from the evaporation of gasoline fumes at gas stations. Under its statutory power to "issue such rules and regulations it finds to be reasonably necessary to protect the human environment," it has issued a notice of proposed rulemaking that states:

> The EPA is seeking to reduce or eliminate the evaporation of fumes at gasoline stations. Many options are being considered, including, but not limited to, a recovery device on automobiles and/or a recovery device on gasoline pumps.

In response to this notice, the EPA received hundreds of comments. Many comments stated that recovery devices on automobiles would be unsafe and expensive and that recovery devices on pumps would be ineffective and expensive. Several comments, from environmental groups, advocated a reformulation of gasoline that would significantly lower the rate of evaporation and thus would accomplish the EPA's goal without any device at all. These comments also argued that gasoline reformulation was the cheapest method of reducing fumes.

After reviewing the comments, the EPA issued a regulation requiring that, within six months, all gasoline sold in the United States conform to the reformulation as proposed in the comments.

The oil companies were not pleased with this action. They claim they did not have adequate notice or opportunity to comment on this regulation. They have filed petitions for judicial review of the regulation in the appropriate federal court. They also have lobbied Congress for statutory relief, and they have lobbied the President to overturn the regulation.

The efforts in Congress failed, but just before the regulation was to go into effect, the President issued an executive order suspending the effect of the regulation "until such time as the EPA conducts a thorough reassessment of the regulation in light of the costs the regulation would impose on the oil industry." Environmental groups and automobile manufacturers have sued the EPA seeking an order that the regulation be enforced as written. They argue that the suspension of the regulation is illegal presidential interference with the EPA's rulemaking authority.

You are a law clerk to the judge before whom both cases have been consolidated. Please write a memorandum with your opinion on the cases. He is most interested in whether the APA has been violated and whether the President's action raises constitutional or statutory issues. Do not worry about whether the oil company challenge is moot—another clerk is working on that issue.

SAMPLE ANSWER TO QUESTION 4 (BASED ON STUDENT ANSWER)

The two biggest issues in this problem are notice and presidential power to order an agency to suspend a regulation and do cost-benefit analysis.

The main notice problem is that the notice of proposed rulemaking did not mention the possibility that the agency would require reformulated gasoline. The only possibilities actually mentioned were vapor recovery devices on gasoline pumps or in cars. The oil companies will argue they did not have sufficient notice. They will stress the purposes of the notice requirement (giving parties a meaningful opportunity to comment and ensuring the agency receives useful information) and argue that neither of these purposes was served, since the oil companies had no idea that reformulation of gasoline was being considered.

In my view, these notice arguments should fail for several reasons. First, the agency was careful to say that it was considering many options, not limited to the ones mentioned. The oil companies should have realized their product might be affected, since it was their product that was causing the environmental problem. Second, the agency complied with the terms of the APA §553. Section 553 requires notice of the terms of the proposed rule *or* the subjects or issues involved. The notice definitely included the subjects or issues involved in the rulemaking. After *Vermont Yankee*, courts should not add to APA procedural requirements, and since the agency complied with §553, there should be no notice issue. Third, basing the argument on the "opportunity to comment" should not help turn a bad notice argument into one based more firmly on the terms of §553. All notice problems affect the opportunity to comment, and as long as the notice meets the notice requirements of §553, a court should not use a different provision to void the rulemaking.

The EPA may argue that based on the language of the statute, the decision of how much to regulate is committed to agency discretion by law. The statute looks like a "deeming clause" in that it says that the EPA should issue regulations that "it *finds* to be reasonably necessary." While in some contexts this might indicate intent to vest the agency with unreviewable discretion, this kind of language is used all the time and is not sufficient to overcome the presumption in favor of judicial review. The statute is a typical regulatory statute and gives plenty of guidance to facilitate judicial review.

There also is a ripeness issue here because the companies want to challenge a rule before it has been enforced against them. They need to meet the fitness and hardship test to get judicial review before agency enforcement. Here, there probably is hardship. Whatever it costs to reformulate, including potential costs to modify refineries and do all the research and testing to make the new gasoline work properly, will cause plenty of hardship. The issue also may be fit for judicial review because there are really no individualized issues, just the question of whether the agency had a sufficient basis to require the reformulation based on the facts in the record and also whether the agency observed all required procedures. It is not a purely legal issue like in *Abbott Laboratories*, but the decision does not vary from company to company based on the situation, so the rule is fit for review at this time.

The second set of issues concerns the President's order suspending the regulation and requiring EPA to reconsider in light of the costs of the regulation. I want to clear away first one issue I think is a red herring—that of ex parte contacts. It could be argued that the oil companies did something wrong by approaching the President outside the notice-and-comment process. I think any suggestion that this was improper should be rejected. In a democracy, contact with elected officials is to be expected and in fact valued. Nothing in the APA limits this type of contact, and it might even be unconstitutional to attempt to prevent the President from having contact with members of the public who are interested in a matter before an agency.

The President's order raises a whole set of interesting questions. First, there is the question of the President's inherent power to supervise the executive branch. The EPA is an executive agency. The President has the power to fire the Administrator of the EPA, and presumably if the President cannot convince an EPA Administrator to delay the effective date of a regulation, the President could fire the person and appoint someone more responsive. If you believe the unitary executive theory, the fact that Congress delegated the authority directly to the EPA should not matter, because any effort to prevent presidential influence is unconstitutional. If you take a more moderate view and hold that the President's power is merely to execute the laws as written by Congress, then you would be more troubled by presidential intervention into the EPA's work. Sure, the President could fire the Administrator, but he may not want to do so for a variety of reasons, and he should not be able to meddle in authority delegated to the Administrator. If Congress has not specifically denied the President the power to suspend regulations, and also has not granted the power, the question falls into Justice Jackson's middle category and raises a difficult, uncertain question. This separation of powers issue is not governed directly by case law, so I am not able here to resolve it authoritatively and leave open the question whether the President has this power.

Coming at the issue from another angle, the question may be whether it violates separation of powers for Congress to delegate power directly to the EPA and not allow the President to directly supervise the EPA's decisions. Unless you believe in the unitary executive theory, this question should be answered under general separation of powers standards, which would ask whether the President's ability to carry out his constitutional role or function as an independent branch of government is threatened. Again, unless you believe in the unitary executive, insulation from direct presidential supervision should be upheld. The President has no interest in enforcing the law except as written by Congress, and this law grants the discretion to the EPA.

There is another serious problem with the President's order. The President ordered the EPA to reassess its decision in light of the costs to the oil industry. The question is whether cost to the oil industry is a relevant factor that the agency should consider. (I am putting to one side the very uncertain issue of whether the President can order the agency to consider a factor that it would prefer not to consider but that may be within a permissible construction of the statute. That issue is subsumed in the discussion above.) The statute says "reasonably necessary to protect the human environment." The use of the words "reasonably necessary" has been held, in the OSH Act, not to require cost-benefit analysis, and the EPA may interpret this to consider environmental protection only and not costs. However, in *Michigan v. EPA*, the Court read similar language to require consideration of costs, so this issue is unclear. If Congress did not intend for the agency to consider costs, then any rule considering them would be arbitrary and capricious for considering an irrelevant factor. The President does not have the power to amend a statute. If a court finds that Congress did not intend for costs to be considered, then the President would not have the power to order the agency to consider them.

There is an argument that as head of the executive branch, the President should have the rather moderate power to order an agency to rethink a regulation in light of issues that the President finds important. Further, it can be argued that since the regulation had not yet gone into effect, it is not a big step for the President to ask for a delay. However, this ignores the fact that the agency had promulgated the requirement as a final rule. In the *Airbags* case, the Court held that an agency could not just throw out a final rule without good reason, and in that case the rule had not yet gone into effect. By analogy, this rule is entitled to all the respect afforded a rule that has actually gone into effect. The President cannot by fiat suspend the operation of a validly promulgated rule.

Finally, standing should be mentioned. The environmental groups would have to establish injury. They can probably do that just by alleging that some of their members breathe the air that is affected by gasoline vapors. The groups would have to meet the requirements for associational standing: Members must be injured, the claim must be related to the association's purpose, and participation of individuals must be unnecessary to resolution of the case. These factors are likely to be present here.

In sum, the EPA probably gave sufficient notice, and the President's order raises serious questions regarding presidential power to supervise agencies.

QUESTION 5

On January 1, 2013, the EPA promulgated final rules sharply restricting emissions from all stationary sources, including all power plants. These new restrictions, which were upheld on judicial review, did not include regulation of greenhouse gases. Compliance was very expensive, especially for coal-fired power plants. On July 1, 2014, in a press release, the EPA announced a new rulemaking initiative that would apply very strict greenhouse gas emissions standards to coal-fired power plants. On August 1, 2014, the EPA published the proposed greenhouse gas rules in the *Federal Register*. The proposal allowed for a six-month comment period, which closed on February 1, 2015. The proposal stated that any final rules would include a one-year delay in implementation to allow regulated plants to be fitted with appropriate emissions controls or to be closed in an orderly fashion. The rule proposed substantial daily fines for noncompliance after the implementation period. Over 1 million comments were received, including many from supporters of the coal industry (who fear that plant closures will reduce their sales) and owners of coal-fired power plants. In addition to many policy-oriented comments, the industry jointly submitted one massive detailed technical comment opposing the proposed rules, which included scientific studies showing that it would take at least three years for most coal-fired power plants to comply with the proposal, and that if the power plants were shut down for modification, there would be serious power shortages and electricity prices would spike. Industry comments also argued that the EPA lacks statutory authority to issue the rules. They supported this claim with detailed statutory arguments. In response to comments, on May 1, 2015, the EPA issued a notice in the *Federal Register* with a slightly modified proposal. The proposal still contained the one-year implementation plan. The EPA's notice stated that comments on the revised proposal would be received for thirty days, and the expectation was that the final rule would be promulgated on September 1, 2015. The EPA's new notice stated that it disagreed with industry's reading of the statute.

On May 5, 2015, members of the coal industry and owners of coal-fired power plants filed what they call an "Emergency Petition for Immediate Judicial Review" in the Court of Appeals for the D.C. Circuit. They claim that the EPA lacks statutory authority to issue the proposed rules and that, to comply, they must immediately start modifying power plants to avoid long closures or fines. You have been asked by the Court of Appeals for your opinion on whether it should entertain this petition at this time and whether the parties have standing to seek judicial review at this time. Be sure to argue both sides.

SAMPLE ANSWER TO QUESTION 5 (BASED ON STUDENT ANSWER)

Because the question asks only whether the court should entertain this petition at this time and whether the parties have standing to seek judicial review at this time, I do not discuss the merits including statutory authority, standard of review, or rulemaking procedures. The fact that the challengers filed their petition in the Court of Appeals raises a question of jurisdiction. If there is no statute specifying that petitions for review of EPA rules should be filed in the Court of Appeals, then the petition should have been filed under the District Court's original federal question jurisdiction. This is not a serious problem, since the Court of Appeals could simply transfer the case to the District Court.

I address timing first and then standing. There are two separate timing issues that need to be addressed: finality and ripeness. The most significant problem with the timing of this petition for review is finality. Simply put, because the rulemaking process is ongoing, the agency's action is not final. Under APA §704, "[a]gency action made reviewable by statute and final agency action for which there is no other adequate remedy in a court are subject to judicial review." This action is not final, since the rule has not yet been promulgated. Merely reopening the comment period with a new notice, even with indications of how the agency is likely to decide, is not a final agency action. Further, the APA states that "[a] preliminary, procedural, or intermediate agency action or ruling not directly reviewable is subject to review on the review of the final agency action." This seems like a preliminary or intermediate agency action and thus is not reviewable under the APA until the agency actually promulgates a rule.

There are arguments in favor of finality. Based on the agency's new notice, it seems pretty clear that the agency is going to promulgate a rule regulating greenhouse gas emissions. The agency explicitly stated that it disagrees with the arguments against statutory authority, and it also seems set to maintain the one-year implementation plan despite the comments indicating that this period is unreasonably short. The short new comment period and promise of a quick promulgation support the argument that the agency action is effectively final. Further, the challengers will have to prepare for compliance now, so the agency's action is already having concrete effects. These arguments may be clever, but they cannot defeat the reality that the agency has not promulgated a final rule, and thus there is no final agency action to review.

Assuming that the court does not find the lack of finality insurmountable, the petitioners might also have a ripeness problem. Because no enforcement action has been taken, under *Abbott Labs*, they would have to demonstrate fitness and hardship. Is the agency's action fit for review at this time? If the only issue is the agency's statutory authority to regulate greenhouse gas emissions from coal-fired power plants, it might be fit for review, although the fact that no rule has actually been promulgated gives me pause on this. (You did not ask this, but under the West Virginia case, under the Major Questions Doctrine, EPA lacks authority to impose a rule that effectively requires replacing coal with another fuel.) What if the agency changes its mind during the next few months and promulgates a different rule or no rule at all? Fitness seems doubtful. The challengers might have a stronger argument on hardship—they allege that compliance will take three years and that they might have to close their plants (and lose lots of business) if they are forced to comply or wait for enforcement before challenging the rule. This is not the sort of hardship in *Abbott Labs* with criminal penalties and terrible reputational harms, but daily fines are substantial, and it's either that or close down—certainly a substantial hardship. Again, however, the fact that no rule has been promulgated undercuts the hardship argument. Maybe the agency won't promulgate the rule or will promulgate a less stringent rule. On the other side, the fact that the agency's new notice seems to stick to its guns supports the idea of immediate hardship.

In sum, I do not believe that there is final agency action, and even if there is, there are substantial ripeness problems with pre-promulgation review (as opposed to pre-enforcement review).

Standing is wrapped up with timing to a certain extent, because if the rule has not yet been promulgated, there is an argument that nothing the agency has done can injure anyone yet. Timing aside, the power plants have a stronger argument for standing than the coal producers, but as long as one of them has standing, the case can go forward. Power plants will certainly be injured by the regulation if they are forced to purchase expensive pollution equipment or even close down. This harm will certainly be caused by the new rules, and invalidation will certainly redress the harm—no rule equals no expense or closure. (This all assumes that it's not too early—there is an argument, captured in the ripeness and finality discussion above, that no injury actually occurs until a rule is promulgated. But the challengers have a logical argument that if it's really going to take three years to comply, they are injured, especially now that the agency has issued its second notice, which indicates that the rule as proposed will be adopted.) As far as the zone of interests test is concerned, the regulated party is always in the zone of interests insofar as the claim is directed at the agency's treatment of the challenger.

The coal producers have a weaker argument for standing because their business losses depend on how the power plants react to the new rules, and they may not be in the zone of interests of a law regulating pollution. If the producers could show that their stock prices are down or, even better, that orders are already down, they should meet the injury requirement. However, the zone of interests test seems very weak, and as long as their interests were at all relevant to the legislative process, they should meet it. It is very likely that energy production was relevant to the shaping of the Clean Air Act. But again, as long as the power plants have standing, the case can go forward.

So, in conclusion, it is doubtful that a challenge to a proposed rule is ripe, and it is doubtful that there has been any final agency action. The case will be final and likely ripe after September, when the final rule is published. The plaintiffs may have standing at this time, but they will certainly have standing when the final rule is issued.

QUESTION 6

The Department of Energy's Battery Agency (BA) has been working on new standards for batteries for electric and hybrid cars since 2009, and it has produced no proposal. In January 2016, the Secretary of Energy appointed a new official to head the BA, Penny Power, who previously was CEO of Penny's Power Company (PPC), a major developer of batteries for electric and hybrid cars. Before taking office, Penny cut ties to the company and sold all of her stock. In February 2016, the BA published in the *Federal Register* a notice of proposed rulemaking that stated simply: "The BA intends to adopt standards governing batteries for electric and hybrid cars. We have no particular proposal at this time and would like specific, technical suggestions on proper battery standards." During the 90-day comment period, Penny had several discussions with her successor at PPC about "how things are going at PPC." Although there is no record of those conversations, Penny denies that they included any discussion of the substance of the rulemaking proceeding. The comment period closed in May 2016. When the final rule was published in September 2016, it created standards favoring PPC's products over those of its chief rivals. The concise general statement of the rule's basis and purpose contained justifications for the rule based on supportive comments in the record, mainly supplied by PPC, and it contained justifications for refusing to adopt competing standards proposed in rivals' comments. PPC's rivals are in front of the federal district court for the District of Columbia, seeking judicial review of the final rule. They argue that the procedure used to promulgate the rule violated APA §553. Please address any procedural issues raised by their petition for review. Do not discuss the substance of the rule or any question about the process of Penny's appointment.

SAMPLE ANSWER TO QUESTION 6 (BASED ON MEMO TO STUDENTS AFTER EXAM)

The main issue in this question is whether the notice was adequate. All the agency said was: "The BA intends to adopt standards governing batteries for electric and hybrid cars. We have no particular proposal at this time and would like specific, technical suggestions on proper battery standards." The text of APA §553 requires the agency to give the terms or substance of the proposed rule or the subjects and issues involved. Clearly, the agency did not give notice of the terms or substance of the rule, but did the agency give the subjects and issues involved? Maybe or maybe not. The notice was very vague. It gave the subject—standards for batteries—but did it give the issues? There is a strong argument that there was no notice of the issues. It might be that everyone in the industry would understand what the issues would be just by knowing the subject. More generally, the notice is arguably so vague that it is not consistent with the purpose of §553's notice requirement, which is to allow interested parties to comment intelligently on the proposal and to protect their interests. A counterargument to this is that the opposing companies commented, so they probably had adequate notice. The logical outgrowth test is also used to determine whether notice is adequate, and here the notice is so vague that perhaps nothing can be the logical outgrowth of it, so any rule flunks the logical outgrowth test.

On the other side, you could turn this argument around and say that since the notice was vague, the rule was obviously the logical outgrowth of the notice. This brings us back to the original argument, that the notice is so vague that it violates the purposes of §553 rulemaking, to give interested persons a genuine opportunity to comment on the proposal. But this may violate *Vermont Yankee's* policy, that for predictability, informality, and agency flexibility, courts should apply only the bare words of §553 and not apply more vague standards like logical outgrowth, etc. *Vermont Yankee* points toward courts not imposing any procedural requirements that are not obvious from the text of §553.

There were also ex parte contacts during the rulemaking, but not ones that would justify invalidating the rule. There is no suggestion that Penny discussed anything related to the merits with her former company, and thus only if you apply a super-strict rule would there be any argument that the rule is invalid due to the communications. The strict rule might be justified by the *Springfield-Sangamon* case—this may appear to be a competing private claim to a valuable privilege, the right among a few battery makers to be certified as following federal standards. But the better answer is that it is a general rule because the facts do not indicate anything about how few battery makers there are, and the rule will govern anyone who wants to make batteries in the future. If these are considered improper ex parte contacts, then the rulemaking should be reopened so that other interested persons can comment on them. But again this is a weak argument since the comments were not really on the merits of anything involving the rulemaking.

A related issue is bias or prejudgment (under the unalterably closed mind test). There is nothing in the facts suggesting that Penny said anything related to the merits of the rulemaking before it was decided, so there is no prejudgment in that sense. There is a good argument that any former CEO is biased in favor of her former company and should not decide any issue vital to that company. Otherwise, there is no real evidence that she would gain anything by deciding in favor of her former company. The communications might support the bias argument because they show she would want to help her friends. If you have friends on one side of a dispute, that might indicate bias. But what is the standard for bias? The unalterably closed mind standard is very difficult to meet, and she does not have any direct pecuniary interest in the rulemaking as far as we know. This smells, but it might not actually be illegal. Further, maybe under *Vermont Yankee*, there should be no standard for disqualification in rulemaking since the APA does not specify this. However, extreme bias in a rulemaking might violate due process, which means that *Vermont Yankee* does not bar considering the questions.

The concise general statement seems adequate based on the characterization in the question, so that is not an issue in this question. In sum, the most promising challenge to this action is that the notice was too vague. Bias, prejudgment, and ex parte contacts are not likely to be successful arguments.

QUESTION 7

Should the Supreme Court extend the prohibition on two levels of for-cause protection from discharge to Administrative Law Judges? Why or why not? Would it make a difference if ALJs could issue only recommended decisions?

SAMPLE ANSWER TO QUESTION 7 (BASED ON MEMO TO STUDENTS AFTER EXAM)

In the *Free Enterprise Fund* decision, the Court decided that it was unconstitutional for an employee to be protected by two levels of for-cause restrictions on removal. This means that any official whose superiors can be fired only for cause must be removable without cause. The Court specifically reserved the question of whether this should apply to ALJs. In my view, the Court should not extend this doctrine to ALJs for several reasons. First, it would cause serious due process problems. The agency decides to bring enforcement actions against regulated parties, and the agency supervises the "prosecutors" in these cases. If the agency heads also have power to remove the ALJs who hear the cases without cause, it looks like a rigged, unfair process. The ALJs would be rightly concerned that if they rule against the agency, they will lose their jobs. This is not a fair hearing. Second, the APA provisions creating removal protections for ALJs have been on the books for nearly 80 years and their constitutionality has never been questioned. This weakens any argument that these provisions are unconstitutional. Third, the absence of for-cause protections from removal might make qualified people reluctant to become ALJs. ALJs typically serve for many years through multiple administrations. Their job security would be in serious question if every time a new administration took office, their decisions would be subject to new political scrutiny.

Finally, there is really no need for this rule to apply to ALJs because ALJs' decisions are always subject to review by agency heads. ALJs' decisions become final only if the agency itself decides not to review or adopts it as its own, depending on the particular agency's statute. The basis for the two-level prohibition is the President's accountability for the actions of agencies, and the President's authority over agency heads seems adequate to maintain accountability for ALJ decisions since the agency head has full power to review them. This last reason becomes even stronger if ALJs can issue only recommended decisions. Although I still think they would be considered "officers of the United States" based on all of the power and discretion they have when presiding over hearings, in such cases accountability for their decisions rests even more squarely on the agency heads. So long as the President can supervise the heads of the agencies, the President does not need authority to supervise ALJs.

SHORT-ANSWER QUESTIONS AND ANSWERS

SHORT-ANSWER QUESTIONS

CHAPTER 1

INTRODUCTION TO STUDYING ADMINISTRATIVE LAW

1. Is administrative law, especially administrative procedure, derived solely from the APA? ____________________

2. What functions do administrative agencies fulfill? ____________________

3. What are the differences between public interest and public choice theories of agency action? ____________________

CHAPTER 2

SEPARATION OF POWERS AND DISTRIBUTION OF ADMINISTRATIVE POWER

4. Congress enacts a statute authorizing the President to grant favorable trade status to a foreign nation on a finding that the foreign nation "meets acceptable standards on human rights" or that favorable trade status is "in the best interests of the United States." Would this statute violate the nondelegation doctrine? ____________________

5. An amendment to the Internal Revenue Code provides that the Internal Revenue Service (IRS) must submit all proposed regulations to the House Ways and Means Committee. If the committee is silent, the regulations go into effect 60 days after submission. If the committee (by majority vote) disapproves of a regulation, then the effective date of the regulation is delayed a further 120 days to allow time to introduce (and possibly pass) a bill disapproving the regulation. Normal procedures regarding presentment to the President, veto, and override apply to this bill. If a disapproval bill does not become law within the 120 days, the regulation goes into effect. Is this a constitutional method of oversight? ____________________

6. Congress passes a statute authorizing the Federal Trade Commission (FTC) to appoint "regional enforcement agents" who are authorized to bring actions in federal district court to seek injunctive relief against unfair and deceptive practices in the marketing of goods and services. Is this a constitutional method of appointing these "enforcement agents"? ____________________

7. Congress passes a statute stating that the President must have good cause before firing United States attorneys and that the Senate may, by a majority vote, reject presidential removal of United States attorneys. Are these restrictions constitutional? ____________________

8. Congress is upset about the way that the President is distributing highway funds, so in its new appropriations bill it provides that the comptroller general has the power to reject allocations of highway funds made by the Secretary of Transportation. Is this provision constitutional?

____

9. Congress is upset with the President's choices for United States attorneys, so it passes (over veto) a statute delegating the authority to appoint United States attorneys to the courts of appeals, each of which would appoint the United States attorneys for districts within their respective circuits. Is that constitutional? ____________________

10. The Federal Emergency Management Agency (FEMA) in the Department of Homeland Security (DHS) needs to hire more claims officers to process claims for disaster relief in the wake of disasters. Claims officers counsel disaster victims on which claims to file and how to file them. They also receive the claims and forward them, with a recommendation, to claims adjusters, who have authority to grant or deny claims. Congress specifies by statute that the Director of FEMA, not the Secretary of DHS, "shall have the authority to hire claims officers." Is this a constitutional appointments process? ____________________

11. The Senate has refused to confirm the President's choice to head the Department of Homeland Security. When the Senate leaves for its annual two-week Easter Recess, the Senate does not receive permission from the House of Representatives to adjourn for more than three days. Rather, it holds pro forma sessions every five days in which one Senator gavels the chamber to order and then within ten minutes gavels the session closed. On the eleventh day of this two-week period, the President makes what he characterizes as a "recess appointment" of his choice for Secretary of Homeland Security. The President includes in his appointment message a statement that the appointment is vital to national security. Is this appointment constitutional?

12. In light of the *Jarkesy* decision, is it still permissible for the CFTC to hear claims brought by customers against brokers for reparations under the CEA and counterclaims brought by brokers to collect money owed due to trading losses by the customer? ______________

CHAPTER 3

THE AVAILABILITY OF JUDICIAL REVIEW OF ADMINISTRATIVE DECISIONS

13. Does the existence of federal question jurisdiction, without an amount in controversy requirement, mean that judicial review is available for all agency action? ____________________

14. Assume Congress enacts a food stamp program that provides for three categories of food stamp assistance: emergency assistance, interim assistance, and regular assistance. Emergency assistance is provided on the day of an application when the applicant establishes, to the satisfaction of a caseworker, that the applicant is in dire need of assistance. Interim assistance is provided within ten days of an application for regular assistance when a caseworker concludes that it is likely that the agency will grant the application for regular assistance. Regular assistance is granted when, after full review, eligibility is established under program guidelines. The statute grants judicial review of denials of interim and regular assistance. The statute does not mention review of denials of emergency assistance. Are denials of emergency assistance reviewable? ______________________

15. Assume the same situation as above except that Congress has provided for review of denials of emergency and regular benefits but not interim benefits. How would the arguments against reviewability differ? ______________________

16. Regarding the same food stamp program, suppose a person files for emergency assistance and then after a week has still not received an answer. Can the applicant obtain judicial review of the failure to answer? ______________________

17. A statute provides that "the Administrator of the Environmental Protection Agency shall, in his discretion, designate those toxic waste sites that shall be given priority treatment" under the laws regulating the cleanup of toxic wastes. Priority treatment means that the site is cleaned up immediately, while normally the EPA delays cleanup while it tries to assign responsibility and recover cleanup costs in advance. A group of neighbors (near a particularly bad toxic waste site) sue the administrator when the administrator decides not to designate the site for priority treatment. Is the administrator's action subject to judicial review? ______________________

18. What would be the proper response to a petition for review filed against the Administrator of the Occupational Safety and Health Administration (OSHA) alleging that "the Administrator has failed to take adequate steps to ensure that all Americans work in a safe and healthful environment as required by statute"? ______________________

19. AT&T is upset that the Federal Communications Commission (FCC) is giving favorable treatment to competitors regarding rate regulation and the tariff-filing requirement. AT&T wants to sue the FCC. Would AT&T have standing to sue?

20. The Department of Homeland Security has revoked all work permits issued under any deferred action program and has issued a rule prohibiting all future recipients of deferral of deportation from working. The State of Illinois has approximately 150,000 residents on deferred action with work permits who are paying state income taxes. Does the State of Illinois have standing to sue the Department to invalidate this change in policy?______________________

21. The Food and Drug Administration (FDA) issues, without notice and comment, a policy statement announcing that it will begin to strictly enforce the prohibition on unapproved uses of approved drugs. Does a physician who prescribes approved drugs for unapproved uses have standing to challenge the policy statement on procedural grounds for failing to use notice-and-comment rulemaking? How would you answer the FDA's argument that the physician is not injured because even if it conducted notice-and-comment rulemaking, it would certainly have adopted the policy statement? ______________________

22. A new federal regulation requires cigarette makers to disclose the ingredients of cigarettes on the package. The penalty for noncompliance is a substantial fine and seizure of all cigarettes in commerce not containing the proper labeling. Can the cigarette makers get immediate judicial review of this regulation upon its promulgation? ______________________

CHAPTER 4

JUDICIAL REVIEW OF ADMINISTRATIVE ACTION

23. The Department of Agriculture decided to create a new method of regulating milk prices. Wanting the widest possible input, it decided to hold public hearings in eight locations around the country. The Secretary of Agriculture and other department officials were present at all eight hearings. The hearings were open to the public, and all attendees were allowed to address comments to and ask questions of the Secretary and the other officials present. After the rule was promulgated under APA §553, a milk producer from Wisconsin challenged the rule as not supported by substantial evidence. Is substantial evidence the proper standard for judicial review? ______________________

24. Does the arbitrary or capricious standard always apply? ______________________

25. The Bureau of Land Management approves a plan to harvest timber on 10,000 acres of federal land. This decision was made informally (there was no rulemaking or adjudication), and the decision was explained in a press release issued by the director of the Bureau. The decision is challenged on judicial review under the arbitrary and capricious test, and the Bureau asks the court to affirm its decision based exclusively on affidavits from the Director and her assistants regarding the basis of the decision. Is this the proper procedure? ______________________

26. On review of the denial of a Social Security disability benefits claim, the agency argues that its doctor's testimony that the claimant was not disabled provides (on its own) substantial evidence to support the claim, and therefore the court need look no further into the record. Is this a good argument? ______________________

27. In determining the number of food stamps to which a claimant is entitled, the statute requires the Department of Agriculture to consider "the resources available to the family unit." The Department has recently decided, in a §553 rulemaking, to change its definition of "family unit" and place children who are unrelated (e.g., stepchildren) in the same "family unit," thus reducing benefits to the step-siblings of children who are receiving child support payments. A claimant, whose claim was denied based on child support payments to a step-sibling, sues claiming that the statute does not allow step-siblings to be included in the same "family unit." What is the standard of review for the definition of "family unit"? ______________________

28. The Environmental Protection Agency (EPA) has, for many years, disclaimed jurisdiction under the Clean Air Act over emissions from wood-burning home fireplaces. In a recent §553 rulemaking, the EPA changed its mind and promulgated stringent emissions standards for home fireplaces, determining that home fireplaces are within the definition of "stationary source" and thus all owners of homes with wood-burning fireplaces must seek a permit from the EPA to use them. On judicial review, the challengers claim that this interpretation is subject to the major questions because it changes a long-standing interpretation, would vastly increase the number of permits EPA would have to grant each year, and would cost homeowners in the aggregate hundreds of millions of dollar in permitting expenses or force them to simply stop using their fireplaces. Does the major questions doctrine apply?

29. In response to revelations that airbags have killed and injured children and smaller adults, the National Highway Transportation and Safety Administration decided, in a §553 rulemaking, to rescind the regulation requiring airbags in all cars. It also allowed those cars already manufactured with airbags to be equipped with on-off switches. The automobile insurers submitted comments, supported by scientific research, urging the retention of the airbag rule. They argued that redesigned airbags which did not deploy with so much force, combined with adjustments to the design of automobile dashboards, would resolve the problem. In its concise general statement, the agency did not mention the comments submitted by the insurers. Are the rescission of the airbags rule and the adoption of the switch requirement arbitrary and capricious? ____________________

CHAPTER 5

AGENCY CHOICE OF PROCEDURAL MODE

30. A local zoning board decides, at a public legislative meeting, to increase the required side yard requirement for all homes built in the town, from six feet to ten feet. This decision was made based on a perception that, in areas of the town where the homes are closer than ten feet from the side property line, the lots look too crowded and property values might be harmed. The board also decides that in areas of special concern for open space, it will require twenty feet. At the meeting, the board members took a map of the town and designated twelve parcels of the approximately one thousand in the town as "special concern for open space," and thus required a twenty-foot side yard for any new development. Do any of the town's property owners have a due process claim against the changes in the side yard requirements?

____

31. A statute prohibits "unfair practices in the sale or leasing of automobiles." The statute creates an agency and gives the agency the power to enforce the statute through an elaborate adjudicatory process. The statute also gives the agency the power "to make rules to carry out the provisions of the statute." Does this agency have the power to make a regulation specifying that turning back the odometer of an automobile is prohibited by the statute? Can the agency then use the regulation to limit the hearing to the issue of whether the automobile seller turned back the odometer without considering whether the process is otherwise unfair?

____

32. Suppose the agency in the above question announces the odometer rule in an opinion deciding an individual adjudication of an alleged violation of the statute and then applies the rule in subsequent adjudications under the Act. Should the agency be required to make the rule in a rulemaking as opposed to announcing it while deciding an individual adjudication?

____

33. A federal statute requires that dealers in dangerous wild animals, such as lions and tigers, have fences around the perimeter of their compounds that are "of sufficient structural strength to contain the animals in the event they escape their primary enclosures." For years, the agency in charge had approved fences of heights six feet and higher. Then the agency issued, without notice and comment, an interpretive rule stating that the fences must be at least eight feet tall. The agency then began revoking the licenses of dealers with fences shorter than eight feet. The dealers could contest the revocation in court by filing for judicial review of the revocation. Is this a proper interpretive rule? ____________________

34. A statute grants the Secretary of Agriculture the power to move agricultural programs from one Department of Agriculture facility to another. After internal study (with no public process whatsoever), the Secretary decides to move a very large research program about corn growing from Wisconsin to Iowa. Should the Secretary have conducted a rulemaking or adjudication?

____

35. In 1990, the National Highway Transportation and Safety Administration (NHTSA) issued an interpretive rule concerning the definition of "passive restraint." Although it was not required, NHTSA employed notice-and-comment procedures before issuing the rule. In 2020, the Occupational Safety and Health Administration wants to revise the rule. Must it use notice-and-comment procedures to change the rule? ____________________

Chapter 6

APA RULEMAKING PROCEDURES

36. The Environmental Protection Agency (EPA) has evidence that gasoline fumes pose a serious air quality problem. The agency issues a Notice of Proposed Rulemaking (NPRM) that identifies the problem and includes the text of a proposed rule that would require a new gas tank assembly on all automobiles. The new gas tank assembly would reduce the fumes that escape during fueling and whenever the gas cap is taken off. Comments from automobile manufacturers and consumer groups convince the EPA that it would be cheaper and just as effective to require the addition of a chemical to gasoline that would reduce the fumes emitted. May the EPA promulgate a regulation requiring the reformulation of gasoline without issuing a new NPRM? ____________________

37. On the same fact situation, assume that officials from General Motors attended a meeting with the Administrator of the EPA during the comment period. At the meeting, the attendees discussed the negative economic effects that would occur if the carmakers were required to modify their gas tanks. Does this provide a basis for challenging the final rule?

____

38. Assume that the Food and Drug Administration (FDA) issues an NPRM that proposes a label on all tobacco products stating, "Tobacco Is a Deadly Poison; Quit Now and Save Your Life." Suppose that evidence surfaces that, in a personal letter to one of his former medical school classmates, the Administrator of the FDA (who has final decision-making authority on the rulemaking) wrote, "I view my mission in life as making business as difficult as possible for tobacco companies so I can save as many people as possible from the effects of tobacco. I will never waver from this mission." Does this provide an argument for disqualifying the Administrator? ____________________

39. Assume the same rulemaking on tobacco products. The manufacturers of smokeless tobacco submit studies showing that their products are far less dangerous than cigarettes. In fact, the studies show that lives would be saved if people were encouraged to switch from cigarettes to their products. Suppose that the Administrator imposes the requirement on all tobacco products. In his concise general statement he addresses the dangers of tobacco in general terms and does not mention the issues raised by the smokeless tobacco manufacturers. Are there grounds for attacking the result? ____________________

40. The Occupational Safety and Health Administration (OSHA) is conducting a rulemaking on safety issues regarding employees who work at computer terminals. There are conflicting OSHA studies on the health effects of exposure to radiation from computer monitors. Interests representing employees present reputable studies showing negative health effects and how a relatively inexpensive modification of computer monitors would help. Monitor manufacturers and interests representing employers present studies showing no negative health effects and that monitor modification would be very expensive and would not eliminate the kind of radiation that the opposing experts say is the problem. OSHA imposes the regulation preferred by employees. On judicial review, the court of appeals states that, given the state of the record, the rule is arbitrary and capricious absent an opportunity for each side to cross-examine the other's experts. Is this a proper ruling? ____________________

41. An agency's organic statute states that the agency, before issuing a rule, "must hold an oral hearing at which interested parties may present argument and evidence." Does this trigger formal rulemaking under APA §§556 and 557? ____________________

CHAPTER 7

AGENCY ADJUDICATION AND DUE PROCESS

42. Congress decides that National Highway Transportation and Safety Administration regulations and state product liability law are not adequate to deal with the problem of defective automobiles contributing to accidents. Therefore, it has passed a statute creating the Automobile Defect Liability Board, an agency within the Department of Transportation. Congress has granted the board authority to adjudicate claims against automobile manufacturers for damages arising out of defective design or manufacture and violations of federal automobile safety regulations. Only a plaintiff may choose to have the case heard by the board. If the plaintiff files a claim to be heard by the board, there is no provision for transferring the case to a state or federal court, unless the board decides that it lacks jurisdiction over the case. The statute provides that "Board orders are enforceable by application to the District Court" and "judicial review of Board orders shall be had under Chapter 7 of the APA." In its first decision, the board ruled that the seats of a particular car were defectively manufactured and that they did not meet federal safety standards. The board awarded $1 million in damages to the plaintiff, who was injured when the car seat came loose from the floor of the car in an accident. On judicial review, the automobile manufacturer argues that the board's jurisdiction is unconstitutional. Is it? ____________________

43. A state statute regulating the employment of guards in a state prison provides that "Guards employed by the Department of Corrections are employees at will and can be terminated whenever, in the sole discretion and judgment of the Director of the Department or her designate, termination will serve the best interests of the Department." Department regulations provide that "prior to terminating the employment of a Guard, the Director or her designate will, whenever possible, meet with the employee to discuss the reasons for the termination and to offer suggestions for alternative employment opportunities." Do prison guards have a property interest in continued employment? ____________________

44. A state statute provides as follows:

> Section 1. Teachers in public elementary schools may not be fired without cause, which means substandard performance, misconduct on the job, or illegal or immoral conduct outside the workplace.
> Section 2. Whether cause for firing exists shall be determined by the principal of the school in which the teacher teaches, with any hearing or other procedure in the sole discretion of the principal.

Is this statute consistent with due process? ____________________

45. A city ordinance provides that police officers may inflict serious bodily harm to subdue any person acting in a disorderly fashion. Mr. Smith has a reaction to a new prescription medication and begins to behave erratically while walking on a public street. The police inflict serious bodily harm while subduing him. When he brings a constitutional claim for damages, the defense argues that, given the local law, he was not deprived of a protected interest. Is this a good argument? ____________________

46. A new President pledges to appoint administrators who are willing to be tough and assess large fines against environmental violators. As part of the plan, the Environmental Protection Agency (EPA) (with presidential approval) adopts regulations allowing the EPA to retain fifty percent of all fines collected. The funds must be used to hire more prosecutors and administrative law judges in order to increase enforcement activity. A chemical manufacturer is prosecuted for violations of the Clean Water Act and is assessed a fine higher than any on record, but still within statutory limits. The manufacturer challenges the fairness of the procedure. What result? ____________________

47. The Federal Trade Commission (FTC) regulates unfair and deceptive trade practices. The FTC Act provides that the FTC has authority, after an adjudicatory hearing on the record, to order businesses to cease and desist from an "unfair and deceptive practice." The FTC conducts a rulemaking and promulgates a rule declaring that "it is an unfair and deceptive practice to represent through advertising, labeling, or otherwise that a product contains a unit of weight, volume, or other unit of measure that has no fixed meaning." The FTC holds a cease-and-desist hearing over Bad Cereal Corporation's claim that its raisin bran cereal contains three scoops of raisins, since no scoop size is specified. At the hearing, the only issue is whether Bad Cereal makes the claim in its advertising or labeling. The FTC refuses to reopen the issue of whether the practice is unfair and deceptive. Bad Cereal argues that this violates its right to a hearing. What result?____________________

CHAPTER 8

SUBSTANTIVE POLICYMAKING IN AGENCIES

48. An agency is required to make all regulations "reasonably necessary to accomplish the goal of safety in federally subsidized public housing." After a widely publicized fire in a housing project that killed several people in apartments where the smoke detector batteries had been removed, the agency proposes a regulation requiring that all such housing contain central, hard-wired fire alarm systems. An interest group of owners of subsidized housing presents a study in the comment period, showing that the requirement's costs would be substantially greater than the benefits in terms of total losses from fires. Is this study grounds for a court rejecting the agency's requirement on judicial review? ____________________

49. An agency proposes to locate a large office building in the midst of a residential neighborhood. The residents are concerned about traffic and other changes to the character of the neighborhood that the office building would cause—including the fact that the government would take several neighborhood stores and a church by eminent domain to make room for the project. Must the agency address these matters in its environmental impact statement (EIS) concerning the project? ____________________

50. Assume that the government includes the information discussed above in its EIS, and the agency decides to go ahead with the building. In its explanation of the decision, the agency acknowledges the substantial effects on the community but decides that, overall, the benefits justify incurring those costs. The agency also rejects proposals to reduce the size of the building on the ground that it would be less convenient for the agency to have offices in two different places. Do these facts present grounds for a court rejecting the project under NEPA?

____

51. A statute grants the President the power to order the Army Corps of Engineers to make emergency repairs to dams and levees after a disaster. Must the Corps address the environmental effects of the emergency repairs in an EIS? ____________________

52. An agency denies an application for welfare benefits on the ground that the applicant earns too much money to qualify. The applicant seeks judicial review, and in his petition he establishes conclusively that the agency erred in calculating his income. The agency responds in its brief in opposition to the petition by pointing out that, under agency regulations, the applicant was ineligible because he had filed prior false applications with the agency. What result?

____

53. Assume that on remand of the above application for benefits, the agency denies the benefits on the ground that the applicant had previously filed false applications. The applicant shows on judicial review that in many prior cases, the agency had granted benefits to people who had previously filed false applications. Is this a reason for reversing the agency?

____

54. A benefits recipient is told by an agency official that his benefits will continue unless he earns more than eight thousand dollars in a year. He earns seven thousand dollars in a year. The agency, relying on valid statutory standards which limit earnings to six thousand dollars in a year, terminates his benefits and informs him of the statutory one-year waiting period for reapplying. Is the erroneous advice he received any reason to invalidate the agency's action?

____

CHAPTER 9

AGENCY ENFORCEMENT AND LICENSING

55. A person living near a large factory is upset that the Environmental Protection Agency (EPA) has not stopped the factory from emitting illegal air pollution. Can the person compel the EPA to bring an enforcement action against the factory owners? ______________________

56. The National Highway Transportation and Safety Administration (NHTSA) is concerned about the safety of rear door latches on minivans. It brings a proceeding against one manufacturer to force it to recall its minivans and change the latches on the rear doors, which NHTSA claims may open in relatively low-impact accidents. The manufacturer claims that all minivan latches are the same and that another company's latches open even more easily than its own. Is this a valid defense? ______________________

57. A new governor appoints a new state Attorney Disciplinary Board composed exclusively of members of large law firms. One of the board's first actions is to announce that it intends to enforce a long-standing (but rarely enforced) ban on practicing law under a trade name. It then issues an immediate suspension notice to four lawyers practicing under the name "The Legal Clinic" and orders them to appear before the board for a hearing to determine whether the board should revoke or suspend their licenses to practice law, and whether an order should issue prohibiting them from practicing under a trade name. Are there any procedural problems with the board's actions? ______________________

58. The Federal Communications Commission (FCC) announces that a new radio frequency is available in Chicago. Two applications are filed for the frequency—one by Michael Jordan and one by Rupert Murdoch. The FCC, without a hearing, awards the frequency to Michael Jordan and denies Murdoch's application on the ground that he already owns the maximum number of radio stations allowed under FCC rules. Murdoch protests that the FCC should have held a comparative hearing before awarding the license to Michael Jordan. Does Murdoch have a valid complaint? ______________________

59. The Secretary of Energy is presiding over a ratemaking proceeding regarding natural gas prices. After the close of the hearings, the Secretary asks the Assistant Secretary within the department directly responsible for overseeing natural gas distribution for an analysis of the natural gas market, with recommendations on rates. Only the Secretary and his staff see this memorandum, and the Secretary adopts most of the rate recommendations contained in the memorandum. Does this procedure provide a basis for a challenge to the rates?

____

CHAPTER 10

AGENCY INFORMATION GATHERING

60. The Occupational Safety and Health Administration (OSHA) has regulatory authority over workplace safety. A resurgence of cigar smoking has OSHA concerned about the second-hand cigar smoke exposure of people who work in restaurants and bars where cigar smoking is allowed. An OSHA inspector arrives at a Chicago Butt and Brew Pub Restaurant (which is part of a national chain of restaurant-bars that promote themselves as cigar-friendly) and informs the manager that he is there to collect air samples in various locations around the restaurant, including "employee-only" areas such as the employee restrooms and employee lounge where employees eat and take breaks. Can the manager refuse entry?

____

61. In the last several years, Los Angeles has seen a substantial increase in the number of illnesses suffered by people who eat raw food in restaurants. The Los Angeles Board of Health decides to inspect, four times per year, all restaurants that serve sushi and all restaurants with salad bars. Further, the rule states that any restaurant that is subject to a complaint of food poisoning should be inspected as soon as possible after the Board receives the complaint. The Board's regulations provide that any restaurant that impedes the inspector from carrying out an inspection shall automatically lose its license and be closed until it allows the inspection. A patron of Billy's Salad and Sushi Bar on Melrose Avenue in Los Angeles contracted a severe case of food poisoning after eating at Billy's. Billy refuses to allow the Board's inspector to enter without a warrant. Does Billy have the right to insist that the inspector obtain a warrant?

____

62. As part of welfare reform, the federal government requires that states, in order to monitor eligibility, conduct regular inspections of the homes of a randomly selected group of at least five percent of the recipients of food stamps and transitional aid to needy families. May state inspectors make consent to such inspections a condition of continued aid?

63. May the government require that all prospective government employees undergo drug tests as a condition for securing government employment? ____________________

64. The president of an insolvent national bank testifies in Congress that he has been unable to locate records regarding a significant number of bad loans, and he blames a former bank employee for the disappearance of the records. Later, the Federal Deposit Insurance Corporation (FDIC), an agency that insures bank deposits, believes that the bank has the records and directs a subpoena to the president of the bank for the bank's records of the transactions. There is a potential for criminal liability of both the bank and the president regarding the transactions and of the president for perjury in his testimony before Congress. Can either the bank or the president resist complying with the subpoena on Fifth Amendment self-incrimination grounds? ____________________

CHAPTER 11

PRIVATE ENFORCEMENT OF REGULATORY NORMS AND PREEMPTION

65. A provision of the Clean Air Act grants a citizens' suit for an injunction against any person, including all government entities, who violates any provision of the Act. The statute also grants an action to compel the performance of a nondiscretionary duty against the Administrator of the Environmental Protection Agency (EPA). The EPA has issued regulations governing second-hand smoke that allow smoking in workplaces as long as sufficient ventilation is in place. The American Lung Association is upset that the EPA did not ban indoor smoking at all workplaces. Can it use the citizens' suit provisions to compel stronger regulation?

____

66. Assume the same citizens' suit provision and the same set of issues. Does the American Lung Association have standing to sue? ____________________

67. A federal statute prohibits gender discrimination at high schools receiving federal funds. The statute specifies that the penalty for failing to maintain equality in all programs is a reduction in federal funds, with a total cutoff if the discrimination continues after initial reductions in funding. The school maintains only one hockey team (a boys' team) and a girl tries out for the team. The coach tells her that the hockey program is not open to girls. She brings suit in federal court against the school district for damages and an injunction to allow her to try out for the team. Her claim is based on a violation of the federal statute prohibiting discrimination in schools receiving federal funds. Is this a proper claim? ____________________

68. A farmer complies with all federal regulations regarding the use of pesticides and fertilizer on his fields. However, the runoff from those fields is causing damage to downstream property owners. For example, it is killing the fish in his neighbor's fishing pond. The affected neighbors sue under state law to have the farmer's use of his property declared a nuisance. They ask for damages and an injunction. Does federal law allow this state law claim to be pressed?

____

69. A worker is fired during a union organizing campaign, and she sues her employer in federal court for violating the National Labor Relations Act by firing her in retaliation for pro-union activities. Can the claim go forward in court? ____________________

CHAPTER 12

LIABILITY OF AGENCIES AND OFFICIALS

70. A naval officer is traveling to his home, which is located off of the naval base, in a vehicle owned by the Navy. The car is part of the Navy's aging fleet of automobiles provided to certain officers. The officer's car is struck head-on by a civilian drunk driver who went through a red light. The officer is seriously injured. He sues the United States Navy under the Federal Torts

Claim Act, alleging that the Navy was negligent for not providing him with an automobile equipped with an airbag. Is this a viable FTCA claim? ____________________

71. The National Highway Transportation and Safety Administration (NHTSA) is charged with developing federal safety standards for automobiles and ensuring that automobiles meet them. Under governing statutes, manufacturers of safety-related automobile parts are required to meet strict standards, and automobiles containing safety-related parts from unapproved manufacturers may not be sold. Global Motors Inc. manufactures a minivan that contains airbags from an unapproved manufacturer. NHTSA knows this but allows the car to be sold anyway. In fact, the airbag manufacturer flunked NHTSA tests and therefore was not certified. May a person, injured when an airbag fails to deploy in an accident, sue the government under the FTCA for injuries due to the government's failure to enforce the statutory safety requirements? ____________________

72. A member of the Federal Trade Commission (FTC) makes a speech in which she criticizes tobacco company executives for pushing deadly drugs on young people. In the speech she argues that tobacco executives should be shunned socially for their contribution to the health problems of the nation. She names the CEOs of the five largest companies, including John Smith. After he became CEO of a tobacco company, Smith ordered the toughest restrictions on company advertising in the industry to keep cigarette advertising away from children. He sues the FTC commissioner under several state law theories, including defamation, tortious interference with contract, and false light. What result? ____________________

73. United States Department of Agriculture (USDA) inspectors obtained a warrant and inspected an egg farm. The inspection revealed numerous violations of USDA and OSHA regulations, some of which affected the safety of the eggs and some of which affected the safety of workers at the farm. The owner of the farm believes that the information that led to the USDA inspectors obtaining the warrants was gathered in an earlier secret inspection of certain portions of the farm. He believes that USDA inspectors broke in at night and then lied on their warrant applications when they stated that they had been tipped off by an informant. Proceedings on the citations are in preliminary stages, and the USDA has acknowledged that if the evidence was illegally obtained, it could not be used against the egg farmer. The owner wants to sue the individual USDA inspectors for damages for violating his constitutional rights. What result?

____

74. Assume the inspectors in the problem above claim that they learned that the egg farmer was about to destroy evidence of serious violations and that there was no time to seek a warrant. Thus, they justify the search based on a belief that they had exigent circumstances allowing a warrantless search. Further, the first federal court opinion on whether exigent circumstances could justify such a search in similar circumstances was not handed down until after the search was conducted. Does this set of circumstances give rise to a defense?

____

75. Assume the same facts as above except, in addition, the administrative law judge rules that the evidence can be used against the egg farm despite the fact that it was seized in violation of the Fourth Amendment. May the administrative law judge be sued under *Bivens* for damages for violating constitutional rights? ____________________

76. Assume a city building inspector denies a building permit without providing a hearing for the applicant. Further assume that due process requires a hearing before the permit can be finally denied. Is the city liable for the damages caused by this violation?

____

CHAPTER 13

FREEDOM OF INFORMATION AND OPEN MEETINGS

77. The National Highway Transportation and Safety Administration (NHTSA) pays a private institute to research the driving habits of owners of sport utility vehicles (SUVs). As part of the study, NHTSA instructs the institute to use a control group of drivers of two sedans, Ford Focus and Honda Accord. An insurance industry group pays the same institute to study seat belt usage in all drivers. The institute, to save money, includes both sets of questions in the same study and uses the same drivers (SUV, Focus, and Accord) for both the driving habits and seat belt usage studies. The institute turns the data regarding SUV drivers over to NHTSA and the data regarding seat belt usage over to the insurance industry group, but keeps the data regarding the driving habits of Focus and Accord owners in its files because of methodological problems with that part of the survey. The institute informs the agency that it will redo that part of the study. A consumer protection and government watchdog organization would like to see all of the data and argues that because government funds subsidized the control group and the seat belt research, all the data belong, at least in part, to NHTSA. Further, the consumer group claims that the Focus and Accord data will show that NHTSA chose the institute because of political favors, not because of the quality of the institute's work. Which, if any, of these data are subject to Freedom of Information Act (FOIA) disclosure? ____________________

78. Cost overruns are plaguing the design and manufacture of a new Army boot. A competitor of the boot maker makes a FOIA request for records related to the design and manufacture of the boot. The Secretary of Defense denies the request, claiming that it would reveal secret national defense records. On judicial review, would the Secretary's denial be upheld?

____

79. A drug addiction advocacy group is trying to gather information on how federal agencies treat employees with drug problems. Are personnel records of employees with drug addiction treatment in their files subject to FOIA disclosure? ____________________

80. A discharged FBI agent seeks judicial review of the agency's decision to fire him. In discovery, he requests files relating to his last ten assignments to show that he performed all assignments competently. He also seeks any communication from the President to the Attorney General and/or to the Director of the FBI. Does the FBI have arguments for withholding this material from discovery? ____________________

81. A member of the Federal Communications Commission (FCC) has lunch with a member of the Council of Economic Advisers. At that lunch, they discuss the economics of the marketplace in digital cellular communications and the likely economic effects of various possible regulatory regimes. Did they violate the Sunshine Act? ____________________

ANSWERS TO SHORT-ANSWER QUESTIONS

1. No. While a great deal of administrative law grows out of the APA, administrative law also has sources in constitutional law (especially separation of powers and due process norms) and in the common law of administrative review that governed before the passage of the APA. The particular statutes governing specific agencies are also important sources of administrative law. With regard to agency procedures, the APA, constitutional due process norms, particular agency statutes, and statutes such as NEPA all contribute to the procedural universe.

2. Administrative agencies distribute benefits, grant permits and licenses, and make and administer policy across a broad range of issues. As government regulation and government benefits distribution have increased, so have the number of agencies and the range of responsibilities of the agencies.

3. Public interest theories focus on the policy reasons for agency action, such as eliminating harmful pollution or redistributing wealth to poor people unable to acquire it in the market or through private charity. Public choice theories focus on the political activity that leads to agency action and are more likely to explain regulation and redistribution as the triumph of powerful interest groups who were able to use political clout to secure benefits for themselves from the legislature or an agency. For example, while public interest theory would explain the regulation of rates in an industry as necessary to keep prices down while ensuring healthy businesses, public choice theory would explain rate regulation as government protecting businesses from competition that would tend to lower their prices.

4. No. Under traditional nondelegation standards, the President's role can be seen largely as "filling up the details." Under the "intelligible principle" test, the requirement that the foreign nation "meets acceptable standards on human rights" is sufficient to pass muster under the nondelegation doctrine. The second half of the statute is a bit more problematic because the "best interests of the United States" standard is not very clear. In some contexts this might raise nondelegation concerns. However, a court might view the statute—invoking the universe of considerations that have long been relevant to Presidents in trade matters—as supplying an adequate intelligible principle. Further, the President's traditional power in foreign relations makes the relative paucity of guidance more acceptable in this context than in other areas.

5. Probably not. The requirements that regulations be submitted to a House committee and that regulations do not go into effect until 60 days after submission are probably constitutional since they do not amount to much of an intrusion into the power of the executive branch and since they become law independent of the action of any unit of Congress. The bicameralism and presentment of the disapproval bill saves it from *Chadha* problems. The constitutionally suspect aspect of the statute is that the vote of the House Ways and Means Committee to disapprove the regulation further postpones the effectiveness of the regulation. Since this action has effects outside the legislative branch of government, it is probably legislative. Thus there would be a violation of *Chadha*'s requirement that any legislative action having legal effect must go through both houses and be presented "to" the President. The argument in favor of the constitutionality of this scheme is that the action of the committee merely delays the effective date of the regulation. The regulation is not canceled without passage of a bill by both houses and presentment to the President; this meets *Chadha*'s concerns.

6. Probably. The answer depends on whether the enforcement agents are inferior officers. A key determinant of whether the enforcement officers are inferior is the degree to which the enforcement agents are subject to the supervision and control of the FTC itself. With no control, the agents might be considered principal officers, although that is unlikely since there is no suggestion that they have policymaking authority beyond the narrow sphere of enforcement. There is even a slight chance that they would be considered "employees" and not officers, although the discretion inherent in enforcement makes this unlikely. Note that under *PCAOB*, the FTC would be considered a department for Appointments Clause purposes, and the commissioners would be considered the heads of that department.

7. One may be, but not the other. The good-cause requirement is probably constitutional; the senatorial role in the removal process is not. Despite the predominant understanding of *Myers v. United States*, Congress has power to impose good-cause restrictions on the President's ability to fire officials exercising executive power. This is made clear from *Morrison v. Olson*, which allowed a good-cause restriction on the firing of an independent counsel. The argument against the good-cause restriction is that by restricting the President's ability to fire a prosecutor with broad prosecutorial powers (including policymaking authority within the district), it infringes unduly on the President's ability to supervise the execution of the law and thus violates the separation of powers. On the Senate's role, the law is clear that Congress, or any unit of Congress, may not itself participate in the removal process. That provision is clearly unconstitutional.

8. No. The comptroller general is removable by a joint resolution of both houses of Congress. Most of the functions of the comptroller general are in aid of the legislative process, and it is thus constitutional for that official to be removable by Congress. However, an official removable by Congress may not exercise authority under the laws of the United States, and this would include the power to disapprove of the Secretary of Transportation's allocation of highway funds.

9. Probably yes. The Appointments Clause allows Congress to grant the power to appoint "inferior officers" to the President alone, to the department heads, and to the courts of law. After *Morrison v. Olson* and *Edmond v. United States*, a United States attorney would probably be considered an inferior officer since the United States attorney is subject to the control of the Attorney General and must follow Justice Department policies. As an inferior officer, the United States attorney is subject to appointment by the courts of law. The two arguments against this statute are: a United States attorney is a principal officer and must be appointed by the President with the advice and consent of the Senate, and the presidential appointment of United States attorneys is necessary to preserve the President's power under a separation of powers analysis. Note that Congress may not grant appointment power for inferior officers to officials not listed in the Appointments Clause and may not itself participate in the appointment of officers of the United States except through Senate confirmation of presidential appointments.

10. Probably yes. Because they lack significant discretion and authority to administer the law, the claims officers would probably be considered "employees," not officers of the United States covered by the Appointments Clause. The contrary argument, based on the Supreme Court's decision in *Freytag,* would be that processing claims and making recommendations involves enough discretion and authority that they are officers covered by the Appointments Clause and thus must be appointed either by the President with the advice and consent of the Senate, or by the Secretary of DHS if Congress so specifies. The D.C. Circuit's *Landry* decision supports the argument that they are employees.

11. Probably not. Under the *Noel Canning* decision, the Senate is not in recess if it says it is in session even if it holds only pro forma sessions. Pre-*Noel Canning*, the Senate would hold those sessions every three days because, by analogy to the Adjournments Clause, it was thought that an intrasession break longer than three days would be considered a recess. However, in *Noel Canning*, the Court stated that an intrasession break shorter than ten days would presumptively not be a recess. Under that reasoning, unless there is some special reason to believe that the Senate was not available to receive messages from the President and act on them for more than ten days, the Senate was probably not in recess, and thus the President could not make a recess appointment. The President's finding that the appointment is vital to national security is unlikely to persuade a court to view this as a recess.

12. Unclear. This is unclear because the Court did not disavow the factors used in *Schor* to determine whether agency adjudication is proper. However, it may be that *Jarkesy*'s historical analysis is meant to displace those factors. In *Jarkesy*, the Court held that parties to adjudicatory hearings that involve remedies similar to those available at common law are entitled to trial by jury, which under well-established legal principles can be held only in an Article III court. However, if the Court were to view the reparations claim brought by the customer as a purely compensatory remedy, language in *Jarkesy* suggests that the jury trial right does not attach and agency adjudication is appropriate. The counterclaim, however, resembles a common-law breach of contract claim and thus might entitle the customer to a jury trial (again unless the Court reaffirms the multifactor analysis it employed in *Schor*). Further, any litigant can waive the right to a jury trial, which implies that agency adjudication is proper when the parties consent by filing their claims and counterclaims in an agency.

13. No. It is important to maintain the distinction between jurisdiction and reviewability. Jurisdiction means that a court may hear a claim, assuming a claim is available. Reviewability is concerned with whether, assuming jurisdiction, a particular agency action can be reviewed. While any claim alleging that an administrator has failed to obey the statute governing her agency may arise under federal law for the purposes of federal question jurisdiction, there are many claims that ultimately cannot be brought because the challenged agency action is unreviewable.

14. Maybe not. There are two sets of arguments against review. First, it can be argued that the denial of emergency assistance is not final since the agency will ultimately decide whether the person is entitled to regular or interim benefits. Against this, it can be argued that the denial of emergency benefits amounts to a final determination that the applicant does not meet the criteria for emergency benefits. The second argument is that by providing for judicial review of denials of interim benefits and regular benefits, Congress has implicitly precluded review of denials of emergency benefits. This argument could be strengthened or weakened with evidence from the legislative history and practice regarding other, similar, programs.

15. Now the arguments against reviewability are much stronger. First, interim benefits determinations look even more like tentative decisions regarding the application than do emergency benefits determinations. Because interim benefits determinations are completely tied to the likelihood that regular benefits will be granted, the decision to deny interim benefits does not seem final. Second, the fact that Congress granted reviewability over one form of temporary relief (emergency) but not another (interim) is strong evidence that Congress did not intend for there to be review of interim determinations. There would be a strong argument that Congress precluded review of interim benefits determinations.

16. Maybe. It can be argued that the failure to answer a petition for immediate, emergency action is ripe for review as a refusal after a reasonable time has expired, and that a week is too long for a response to a petition for emergency food aid.

17. Probably not, on the grounds that the agency action is committed to agency discretion by law. First, the statute does not contain a standard under which the administrator is supposed to decide which sites are given priority treatment. Thus, there may be "no law to apply." Law to apply may, however, be found in the goals of the cleanup program as a whole. Second, the statute explicitly places the priority status determination in the "discretion of the Administrator." This provision may be a "deeming" clause under which judicial review is precluded. Third, it can be argued that this is a decision like prosecutorial discretion because it involves a delicate and expertise-laden balancing of the priorities of the agency. Thus, it is in a category of determinations that are traditionally unreviewable.

18. The court may, under *Norton v. Southern Utah Wilderness Alliance*, dismiss the claim because the claim does not identify "agency action" with sufficient particularity to merit judicial review.

19. Probably yes. Under the legal right test, AT&T would not have had standing because AT&T has no legal right to have its competitors regulated properly. However, under *Data Processors*, AT&T could have standing if it could show that it is injured by the agency action and that it is within the zone of interests in the sense that competitors' interests are relevant to the regulatory scheme governing long-distance telephone service. Since AT&T is in direct competition with the other companies, AT&T is probably injured by a loosening of regulatory requirements on its competitors. The trickier question is whether competitors' interests were relevant when the system of rate regulation was established. It is likely that such interests were relevant so that AT&T would meet the zone of interests test and have standing to challenge the FCC's treatment of its competitors.

20. Probably. Even though the action is directed at third parties, the state would be injured by the loss of tax revenue, and reinstatement of the right to work would remedy that injury. Further, under *Texas v. United States,* the state may receive "special solicitude" when its sovereign interests are affected by federal regulation. However, there are good arguments against standing. For one, the State would be asserting third party rights—the right of deferred action recipients to work, not its own right to collect taxes. Additionally, the deferred action recipients themselves should be able to assert their own rights, perhaps with the aid of advocacy groups. Note: even if there is some other bar to judicial review or the State would have a weak case, standing should be determined independently from other possible impediments to Illinois succeeding in the litigation.

21. Yes, the physician should have standing to challenge the policy statement. The physician is injured in fact because the agency is telling her not to prescribe medications that she would like to prescribe to her patients. Under accepted standing principles, parties may challenge procedural violations even if they cannot prove that the agency decision would have been different had proper procedures been employed. (Note that even if the physician has standing, the agency might have a good argument that the claim is not ripe unless and until it takes action against the physician for an alleged violation.)

22. Maybe. The question is whether the case is ripe for review. In *Abbott Labs*, the Supreme Court decided that a regulation can be reviewed pre-enforcement if the issue is "fit" for review, and the regulated party would suffer substantial "hardship" if review were postponed. Here, the issue is probably fit since the only issue is likely to be whether the agency has the legal authority to impose the rule. There is also probably sufficient hardship since printing the labels would be expensive and reveal information that the company would prefer to keep secret. Further, a substantial fine and destruction of stock without proper labels would also be sufficient hardship.

23. No. Despite Supreme Court dicta to the contrary, the proper standard of review of rules promulgated pursuant to APA §553 is the arbitrary or capricious standard of APA §706(2). The fact that the department held public hearings does not change this because the substantial evidence test applies only to rules made pursuant to APA §§556-557 and rules made "on the record after hearing" (not to rules made pursuant to §553 even if the agency elects to hold informal public hearings of the sort held in this case). "On the record after hearing" means rules made pursuant to a trial-type procedure, not §553 procedures augmented with public hearings.

24. Yes. Some of the standards of review enumerated in APA §706 contain explicit textual limitation on when they apply, while others do not. The arbitrary and capricious test contains no such limitation, which means that it applies to all reviewable agency action. However, because the arbitrary and capricious test is the most deferential APA standard of review, the person seeking judicial review will always prefer to have another, less deferential, standard apply—such as the substantial evidence test or de novo review.

25. No. The court should review the record that was before the agency at the time the decision was made. APA §706 instructs reviewing courts to look at the "whole record" that was before the agency. It is a principle of administrative law that agency action must stand or fall based on the record that the agency considered when it made its decision. Even when the decision is made informally, courts should first look at the actual material the agency considered when it made its decision and should receive affidavits regarding the decision-making process only when the administrative record does not adequately reveal the basis for the agency's decision.

26. No. Under APA §706, the reviewing court is instructed to review the whole record, not merely those parts of it that support the agency. If there was enough evidence (especially documentary evidence), contrary to the agency's doctor's testimony such that a reasonable person would not accept the agency's conclusion, then the agency's decision would not be supported by substantial evidence. This reverses the pre-APA practice under which some courts looked only at the evidence supporting the agency to determine whether the agency's decision was supported by substantial evidence. However, the Supreme Court has made it clear that an expert's testimony, even without revealing underlying data, may constitute substantial evidence for an agency's decision.

27. Historically, there have been two competing traditions. On one view, issues of law are for courts to resolve—with perhaps some moderate deference to the agency's view. The other tradition, exemplified by the *Hearst* and *Skidmore* cases, is for more deferential review, especially when the issue involves agency expertise. Most recently by overruling *Chevron* the Supreme Court has embraced the view that issues of statutory construction are for the courts to decide with some deference to agency views under the *Skidmore* factors. Some members of the Supreme Court would insist that only the plain meaning of the statute should be consulted on this question; others would look more broadly into traditional tools of statutory interpretation such as statutory structure and legislative history. Under prior law, since there is no definition of "family unit" in the statute, the Court would have likely applied *Chevron* step two, under which the Court would ask whether the agency's definition is a permissible construction of the statute. This was a very deferential standard, but, as noted, it is no longer the law.

28. The major questions doctrine probably does not apply to this action, but it is not totally out of the question. There are two arguments against agency action: first, that the agency has newly discovered regulatory authority in a long-extant issue; and, second, that this rule would subject millions of new sources to a permitting requirement, potentially overwhelming the agency. However, requiring permits for home fireplaces does not regulate a significant portion of the economy, does not implicate massive expenditures in the hundreds of billions of dollars, and is not a matter of great political controversy. Thus, although there are serious doubts over whether the EPA would have authority to promulgate a rule like this, application of the major questions doctrine is unlikely (and probably unnecessary.)

29. Possibly. To argue that they were arbitrary and capricious, the challengers should urge the court to carefully review the record before the agency. It appears that the agency's decision is arbitrary and capricious because the agency did not consider alternatives to complete rescission, and it did not adequately explain its decision. The agency unnecessarily gave up the lifesaving benefits of airbags that supported its initial requirement without considering a less drastic alternative and without explaining why it concluded that the lower-force airbags were not sufficient to solve the problems and preserve safety. Further, the agency did not explain why both rescission of the dual airbags requirement and the on-off switch were necessary, and may not have considered the alternative of the on-off switch only.

30. Maybe. The legislative process is fine for the owners of most of the parcels in the town since the decision was made to increase the side yard requirement based on general considerations (legislative facts), and it was applied to all property owners across the board. The owners of the twelve parcels that were singled out for special treatment have a good argument that due process requires that they be given notice and a hearing. The relevant facts look like adjudicative facts. Under the *Londoner* case, an adjudicatory hearing may be required as a matter of due process.

31. Probably yes on both questions. Although the legislature may have intended that the definition of unfair practices would be developed in the course of adjudications, the statute grants the agency power to make rules. Even if the statute appears to grant the power to make procedural rules and not substantive rules, courts are usually very willing to recognize rulemaking power because of the policy advantages of rulemaking over case-by-case policymaking in adjudications.

32. No. There are federal agencies, such as the NLRB, that often announce new rules in the course of adjudication. This practice has been justified on two grounds, against the argument that the APA requires that rules be made in rulemaking. First, it is within the traditional adjudicatory process for rules to be announced in opinions and then to be applied as binding precedent in subsequent adjudications. Second, in the subsequent adjudications, the rule will be applied only in the context of an order directed against the subject of that particular adjudication. As long as all the procedural rights of the subject of the subsequent adjudication are observed, the order is proper.

33. No. If the eight-foot requirement is treated by the agency as binding, it is a new legal requirement—not merely a reminder of what the statute itself always required because the statute does not set forth a height requirement. The agency will argue that the eight-foot requirement merely interprets the meaning of "sufficient structural strength to contain the animals," but this is a weak argument, because there is no way to get to the eight-foot requirement by interpreting the meaning of "structural strength." In any case, because an interpretive rule is not a binding norm, the agency should have to defend its interpretation on judicial review or in enforcement actions. The agency's interpretation would not bind the courts but it might receive deference.

34. No. Unless the governing statute indicates otherwise, the Secretary was free to make the decision without a formal procedure because it is not a rule and because the decision does not focus on the conduct or rights of an individual such that adjudication would be required. There is also an argument that §553 does not apply because the decision is about agency organization. There are many situations in which agencies make decisions informally (i.e., without a rulemaking or adjudicatory process). In response to any complaints from Wisconsin, the Secretary is required, by APA §555(e), to provide a statement of the reasons for the decision.

35. Probably not. Agencies are not required to employ notice-and-comment procedures to issue interpretive rules, even when the interpretive rule changes a long-standing, previously issued interpretive rule. *Perez v. Mortgage Bankers Assn.*, 575 U.S. 92 (2015). Agencies are free to provide more procedures than legally required, but they are not bound to do so simply because they have done so previously. However, a court could conclude that by providing notice and comment in the initial rulemaking, the agency converted what might have been considered an interpretive rule into a substantive, legislative rule. It is not clear whether this view is a correct application of the APA.

36. Probably not. Oil companies will argue that the NPRM did not give adequate notice that reformulation of gasoline, instead of redesign of automobile gas tanks, would be considered. For notice to be adequate, the final rule must be the logical outgrowth of the proposal; the final rule must not be a material alteration of the proposal. The purpose of the notice requirement is to ensure that interested parties know when their interests are at stake, and the oil companies would argue that they had no idea that their product would be the subject of the rulemaking. If the NPRM had mentioned the possibility of other solutions, including reformulation of gasoline, then the oil companies' argument would be weaker. Nevertheless, the oil companies could still argue that absent more specific notice, the EPA should be required to issue a new NPRM focusing specifically on gasoline. However, if the reviewing court applies a more literal reading of §553's notice requirement, it might uphold the notice as adequate because it apprised the public of the subject of the rulemaking—gasoline fumes.

37. Possibly. Even though §553 does not address them, ex parte contacts are frowned on in the rulemaking process. Some courts, on a variety of legal theories, have held that administrators should not willingly receive ex parte contacts; if they do receive them, they should place them on the record for other parties to comment on. In this case, if the ex parte comments were not part of the record (so that opposing interests had no opportunity to comment on General Motors' assertion that there would be a negative effect on carmakers, and that fact was important to the agency's decision), then there would be a strong argument that the agency should reopen the comment period to allow additional comments on that issue. However, some lower courts have held that ex parte contacts are allowed unless they are statutorily banned, and it violates *Vermont Yankee* to bar them without a statutory basis. Note that the regulation of ex parte contacts is less strict here than in adjudication, where ex parte contacts are strictly forbidden.

38. Maybe. The tobacco companies could argue that the Administrator has an "unalterably closed mind" in his mission against tobacco and that he should thus be disqualified from deciding the rulemaking. Note, however, that there is no mention of bias in informal rulemaking in the APA. *Vermont Yankee* might thus argue against judicial power to disqualify the Administrator on such grounds, unless the tobacco interests could convince the reviewing court that their due process rights were being violated. In addition, this issue raises the conflict between legal norms (which might counsel against allowing someone with such strong views to make a decision like this) and political norms (which favor strong views and a record of accomplishment with regard to those views).

39. Yes. The concise general statement should address the major issues raised by the comments. This is an important safeguard against arbitrary decision-making. Here, the smokeless tobacco manufacturers raised a significant issue distinguishing their product from other tobacco products, and the Administrator should have explained why he rejected their arguments.

40. No. Despite the court of appeals' attempt to link its ruling to the adequacy of the record, the decision violates *Vermont Yankee*, which holds that courts may not impose procedures in addition to those specified by the APA. Here, APA §553 does not provide for cross-examination, and as long as the agency has a rational basis for accepting one side's studies over the other's, the rule should stand.

41. No. Formal rulemaking is triggered when the agency is required to make rules "on the record after opportunity for an agency hearing." The statute here does not appear to require that the decision be made "on the record," so even though the statute might create a statutory hybrid, in that an oral hearing must be held, the agency is not required to use formal rulemaking.

42. Probably not. This raises a close question under Article III, but a clearer question under the Seventh Amendment's jury trial right. On the Article III issue, the Board's jurisdiction is over a private rights dispute, in the core of traditional Article III jurisdiction. It is, however, closely related to an area of comprehensive government regulation. In favor of the statute's constitutionality under Article III is that federal courts have concurrent jurisdiction—except that a defendant brought before the board has no choice of forum. Also, the board does not have all the attributes of a district court since its orders are not self-enforcing. The deferential standard of judicial review stands against constitutionality. NHTSA regulations may be comprehensive, but the branch of the Board's jurisdiction over defective designs is pure products liability law and is traditionally a matter of state law, which undercuts the case for administrative adjudication and appears, under *Jarkesy*, to entitle the subject to a jury trial that must be conducted in an Article III court.

43. No. The statute does not create an entitlement. Further, procedures do not normally create entitlements, and here the right to procedure is qualified anyway. The only hint of a property interest is the "best interests" standard. However, that standard is vague, and the statute makes it a subjective standard of the sort not generally found to create an entitlement. Barring other promises, or a long-standing practice of termination only for cause, there is no property interest in continued employment.

44. No. Section 1 creates an entitlement (i.e., a property interest) to continued employment. A teacher may not be deprived of this interest without due process of law. Section 2 is unconstitutional because, under federal due process law, a hearing is required before the principal may fire a teacher, and the hearing must address whether the standard for cause is met. The amount of process required is determined using the *Mathews v. Eldridge* balancing test, which requires balancing the employee's interest in keeping the job and the accuracy-enhancing value of additional procedure against the government's interest in proceeding without additional procedure. In employment cases, that balance ordinarily requires a hearing in advance of firing. Insofar as section 2 purports to require less than constitutionally adequate procedures, that section is unconstitutional. The argument that claimants should have to take the "bitter" of section 2 with the "sweet" of section 1 was rejected by a majority of the Court in *Arnett v. Kennedy*.

45. No. Not all protected interests are determined using entitlement theory. Some such interests are created by the Constitution itself, including the liberty, or Fourth Amendment limitations on the use of force in arrests. Thus, Mr. Smith's constitutional rights may have been violated even though local law does not create an entitlement to be free from excessive force.

46. Based on these facts, it is unlikely that a court would find any procedural problem. There is no allegation that the administrative law judge had any personal pecuniary interest in the outcome of the case, and it is unlikely that the fines collected contribute a high percentage of the EPA's budget. If the ALJ's continued employment depended on large fines, then perhaps a bias claim would succeed. There is also no indication that the ALJ is under explicit pressure to rule against violators or impose large fines, although implicit pressure may be problematic. There is also no direct evidence of prejudgment, and unless the ALJ had made a statement regarding the particular case, it is unlikely that a prejudgment claim would be sustained.

47. As long as the FTC has rulemaking authority, and the rule is not ruled arbitrary and capricious on judicial review, the rule may serve to limit the issues at the hearing. Thus, Bad Cereal's objection should be rejected. However, Bad Cereal must be allowed the opportunity to establish that the rule should be waived (e.g., by bringing forward evidence that all advertisements and labels show the actual size of the scoops) or that everyone knows that the claim is meaningless. These arguments are likely to fail.

48. Probably not. Traditionally, agencies have not been required, by general "reasonableness" language, to regulate only when justified by cost-benefit analysis. Perhaps cost-benefit analysis would be required under current law if the statute included "reasonably necessary and *appropriate*" rather than simply "reasonably necessary." Of course, cost-benefit analysis would be required if the statute clearly required it (e.g., by stating that the agency "may impose a requirement only when the benefits achieved by the requirement are greater than the costs of imposing the requirement"). However, under accepted principles, the agency may be required to explain why it chose to impose the requirement when costs may outweigh benefits and the agency may, if it chooses, reject the requirement on the grounds that it is not cost-effective.

49. Yes. These are actual effects on the human environment that must be addressed in an EIS. The disruption of the social structure of the neighborhood is the sort of impact that must be addressed in the EIS.

50. No. NEPA does not impose a substantive requirement that agencies minimize the environmental effects of their actions. To comply with NEPA, agencies must prepare an adequate EIS and consider the environmental effects in making their decisions. Here, the agency appears to have considered the environmental effects of its proposal. Even though agency convenience may appear to be a rather weak reason to incur substantial environmental damage, the agency has met its NEPA obligations.

51. No, because the matter is in the control of the President, not the agency. An agency is not required to address environmental effects of actions over which it has no control.

52. The court should remand the matter to the agency because in general, on judicial review, the agency may defend its decision only on the grounds relied on in its initial denial.

53. Yes. The agency may have an obligation to treat like cases alike. If the current case is different from prior cases, or if the agency has decided to change its policy, it must explain either the differences or the reasons for the change.

54. No. Agencies are not estopped by the representations of their officials, especially when the result of estoppel would be to pay money from the treasury in violation of the restrictions placed on such payments by Congress.

55. Not unless there is a clear statutory provision requiring the EPA to act on this type of complaint. Agencies normally have a great deal of discretion in choosing how to use their enforcement resources. If a person petitions the agency to bring an enforcement action and the agency denies the petition, the denial may not be subject to review because courts hold that most enforcement decisions are "committed to agency discretion by law."

56. Probably not. Unless the manufacturer can show that the failure to bring enforcement actions against other makers of minivans has no articulable basis, it is no defense to an enforcement action to claim that enforcement should be brought against a competitor as well. The legal standard is "patent abuse of discretion." Because the manufacturer is unlikely to be significantly injured in its ability to compete with other minivan makers, any discriminatory enforcement claim is likely to be very weak. An agency is normally free to proceed one company at a time. The most successful discriminatory enforcement claims are those that raise equal protection concerns, such as a pattern of enforcing regulations against a particular racial group—but even claims like that are difficult to sustain.

57. Yes. First, the immediate suspension without a hearing may have violated due process. Occupational licenses are usually property under the *Roth* line of cases, and due process may require a hearing before an agency may suspend a license unless there is evidence of an immediate threat to public health or safety. Further, the composition of the Board presents a problem under *Gibson v. Berryhill* although perhaps not a serious one. If the Board is dominated by lawyers who do not practice under trade names, and they are attempting to destroy competition from another segment of the profession, then there is a problem. They may be biased because of self-interest in the outcome of the hearing. However, it is not clear that the Board is actually in a different market segment from the firms using trade names. This regulation applies to all lawyers, and thus the Board members are limiting their own activities by enforcing this rule. Further, the big firms may not be in competition with this "legal clinic," and thus the members of the Board may have no personal interest in the outcome. There may be no client of the Legal Clinic who could afford to hire a big firm lawyer.

58. No. While Murdoch is correct that in normal circumstances the FCC must hold a comparative hearing to award a new license among competing applicants, the FCC may promulgate substantive licensing standards and deny applications that, on their face, fail the standard. Here, if the limit on the number of stations is part of a valid regulation (and there is no dispute that Murdoch owns more than the maximum), the FCC may deny his application without a hearing and award the frequency to the competing applicant. However, if Murdoch's application raises a potentially valid ground for waiving the rule in the particular case, the FCC must provide Murdoch with a hearing on that argument and must explain why it has rejected the argument. Recall that the 1996 Telecommunications Act eliminates the comparative hearing requirement for contested renewals.

59. Maybe. The ratemaking process is normally formal adjudication. Here, the Secretary relied upon evidence and analysis that was not part of the record of the proceeding, which is not allowed in formal adjudicatory hearings. Note that the Secretary did not violate the ban on ex parte communications since that ban applies only to "interested persons outside the agency." The Assistant Secretary is clearly not "outside the agency."

60. Yes, unless OSHA has a warrant. The first question is whether OSHA has the legal authority to inspect the restaurant, which it probably does as part of its broad workplace safety mission. That mission includes health issues such as the effects of second-hand smoke. The OSHA inspector probably needs a warrant to compel the manager to admit him to the premises since, as to OSHA workplace safety issues, the restaurant is not a pervasively regulated business. However, if OSHA's desire to inspect the restaurant is part of its routine monitoring of workplace safety, then it can probably obtain a warrant without showing that it has reason to believe that the restaurant is violating OSHA standards.

61. Possibly. Restaurants have not been regarded as "pervasively regulated businesses" with regard to Board of Health inspections for proper food-handling practices, so under normal circumstances a warrant may be required. However, the government's interest in regulating restaurant food handling is substantial, and when there is a documented case of food-borne illness, a warrantless search may be necessary to ensure that evidence is preserved. A counterargument is that a warrant ought to be quick and easy to obtain: the regulatory scheme's program of regular inspections, and inspections after a complaint, provide the safeguards against arbitrary searches that would otherwise be provided by a more onerous warrant procedure. As long as the inspection is part of the normal Board of Health regulatory program, a warrant for an inspection should be easy to obtain. There is also an argument that warrantless searches are necessary to prevent restaurants from "cleaning up" for inspection day but thus far, only pawn shops, firearms dealers, alcohol sellers, mines, and junkyards have been held to be subject to warrantless inspection as pervasively regulated.

62. Probably yes. The Court has allowed such requirements in the past. In the particular case, *Wyman v. James*, the Court relied in part on the rehabilitative nature of the home visits, which involved childcare issues. Here, the only purpose is to monitor eligibility, which puts the inspector in a purely adversarial relationship with the recipient. Nevertheless, if the only consequence of not allowing the inspection would be a benefits cutoff, the Court would likely uphold the requirement.

63. Probably not. The Court has upheld drug-testing programs when there was a special need for the tests, but it struck down a requirement that candidates for statewide office undergo drug testing. For many government positions not involving law enforcement, and where drug abuse would not endanger the public or other employees, the Court would likely hold that the need to be certain about drug abuse was not strong enough to outweigh the prospective employees' privacy interests.

64. No. The bank, as a corporation or collective entity of some sort, has no right against self-incrimination. The Fifth Amendment right against self-incrimination protects only natural persons. The bank president, as custodian of corporate records, may not assert his own Fifth Amendment rights even though the act of producing the records amounts to testimony that the records exist, which directly incriminates him of perjury.

65. No. The provision allowing injunctions against violators applies to the government only when the government itself is polluting, not when the government allegedly is not regulating properly. Unless the statute requires EPA to ban indoor smoking at workplaces, the Administrator does not fail to fulfill a nondiscretionary duty by not banning smoking in indoor workplaces. Only judicial review may be used to attack the substance of regulations.

66. Possibly, but it would have to be based on injury to a member of the Association. If a member works in an indoor workplace where smoking is allowed, then the Association has standing to assert its member's claim. There should be no zone of interests problem as long as the Association's member is a worker, since it is likely that workers are within the zone of interests of the statute. Further, even if there were a theoretical zone of interests problem, the typical citizens' suit provision places everyone identified as having a claim within the zone of interests.

67. Maybe. The Supreme Court has approved a private right of action under statutes like the one described, largely because the plaintiff is clearly within the class of people who benefit from the statute, and the private action would tend to advance the purposes of the statute. However, in the absence of evidence of congressional intent to allow the private right of action, the courts today would be skeptical of the claim. The Supreme Court now appears to agree with Justice Powell's dissent in *Cannon* that judicial creation of a right of action out of a regulatory statute raises serious separation of powers concerns on the ground that it is for Congress to decide whether to create a federal cause of action.

68. Probably yes. The federal statute probably regulates the safe use of pesticides and fertilizers because of safety and general environmental concerns. Such statutes often have savings clauses and rarely preempt state tort law. The federal statutes that regulate the labeling of pesticides have been held not to preempt state claims based on improper use of pesticides. However, if the federal statute explicitly preempts claims based on the use of pesticides and fertilizers, or if the overall context indicates that Congress intended to preempt such claims, then the state claim might not survive.

69. No. A claim that an employer has fired an employee for engaging in pro-union activities states a claim that the employer has committed an unfair labor practice. Such claims are within the primary jurisdiction of the NLRB; it is up to the Board to determine whether the company has committed an unfair labor practice.

70. No, for several reasons. First, under the *Feres* doctrine, members of the military may not sue over decisions of their superior officers even if the FTCA might otherwise provide for liability. Second, because the decision involved discretion and choice, the FTCA's discretionary-functions exception bars liability. Third, under state law, it may not be tortious to provide an employee with an automobile without an airbag. Thus, even if the other obstacles to FTCA liability could be overcome, the predicate for FTCA liability (liability for similar conduct under local law) would not be met.

71. Possibly. The Supreme Court has rejected a "regulatory functions" exception to the FTCA, so even though the government is playing a purely regulatory role, the FTCA might still be available. If NHTSA approved the car in violation of clear statutory directives, then the discretionary-function exception would probably not bar liability. The *Berkovitz* Court held that there is no discretion to violate mandatory provisions of governing law. However, the plaintiff must establish that the approval of the automobile did not involve choice or policy judgment—that there was no discretion regarding observance of the statutory requirement.

72. The suit would likely be unsuccessful. Federal officials have immunity from damages for common-law claims based on conduct within the outer bounds of their official duties. It is within the outer bounds of the duties of FTC commissioners to speak on matters of public interest involving advertising, which is within FTC jurisdiction.

73. He probably has a viable *Bivens* claim against the inspectors. Under *Bivens*, victims of Fourth Amendment and other constitutional violations can sue the perpetrators for damages. Even though the exclusionary rule might prevent the use of the evidence in the agency proceedings, it is not a substitute for a damages remedy against the offending officials. Congress has not declared that the USDA procedures are a substitute for the *Bivens* action, and the fact that the USDA applies the exclusionary rule in its proceedings is not enough to make the existence of those proceedings a "special factor counseling hesitation." While a comprehensive remedial scheme might be a special factor, here the USDA scheme does not really provide a remedy for the Fourth Amendment violation, so it should not displace the *Bivens* action.

74. Yes. They may have a qualified immunity defense. Under qualified immunity, officials are not liable unless they violate clearly established constitutional rights of which a reasonable official should know. If the inspectors establish that no similar case had found a Fourth Amendment violation, they would be immune from a damages award. Note that it is not enough that the general right to be free from an unreasonable search and seizure is clearly established. The cases require that it be clearly established that the particular facts alleged establish a constitutional violation.

75. No. The ALJ has absolute immunity from damages for constitutional violations in performance of her judicial duties. At common law, judges, legislators, and prosecutors had absolute immunity from damages. Under the functional approach, administrative officials are accorded the same immunities as their nonadministrative counterparts. ALJs thus receive judicial immunity, agency prosecuting officials receive prosecutorial immunity, and agency officials making rules receive legislative immunity.

76. Maybe. Municipal liability in this situation depends on many factors. While cities are proper defendants in §1983 cases, they cannot be held liable on a vicarious liability theory. Rather, cities may be held liable only for violations attributable to municipal policy. If the city had an official policy requiring hearings before denials of building permits, then the city cannot be held liable. However, if city policy stated that no hearing was required, or if the building inspector had the final authority under city law to determine whether a hearing would be held, then it would be appropriate to hold the city liable for damages.

77. NHTSA is an agency, and any data turned over to it would be considered part of agency records since they would be obtained by the agency for agency purposes. Thus, the data regarding SUV driving habits would be subject to FOIA disclosure unless further information would reveal that some exemption should apply. The remaining data are likely not to be subject to FOIA disclosure because the data are not in government files. Even if NHTSA has a right to obtain the data, courts have held that FOIA does not obligate agencies to obtain files to make them subject to public disclosure. Thus, even though an important FOIA-related purpose would be served by publication of the flawed Focus and Accord data, because those data are not part of agency records, they are not subject to FOIA disclosure.

78. No, unless the records were properly classified. Records may be withheld as secret national defense records only if the records have been classified as secret pursuant to executive orders creating and regulating the classification system. *See* 5 U.S.C. §552(b)(1). Thus, unless the boot records were properly classified as secret defense records pursuant to an executive order, the Secretary may not withhold them as secret defense records under FOIA.

79. Maybe. Exception (6) exempts from disclosure "personnel and medical files and similar files the disclosure of which would constitute a clearly unwarranted invasion of personal privacy." The test for whether an invasion of privacy is "unwarranted" is a balancing test with the interests in monitoring government activity on one side and the individual's privacy interests on the other. Raw data, without names and other identifying factors attached, would pose very little risk of invasion of privacy and thus might be available under FOIA. Any information, however, that might lead to identification of drug-addicted federal employees would not be subject to FOIA disclosure.

80. Yes. The FBI may have an evidentiary privilege if it can show a judge that release of the material would damage important law enforcement interests. Further, the FBI might assert executive immunity to resist revealing the contents of any communication from the

President to the Director of the FBI. On the claim of executive immunity or privilege, once the claim is made, the party seeking the material has the burden of establishing that the material is vital to achieving justice in the proceeding. The plaintiff's interest in obtaining the material is substantial but is not as weighty as the interest of a criminal defendant's in obtaining material important to defending a criminal prosecution.

81. No, because the lunch was not a meeting of an agency. A meeting constitutes a meeting of an agency only when there is a possibility that agency business will be conducted. There is no suggestion that a single FCC commissioner or a single member of the Council of Economic Advisers has the power to conduct agency business alone.

MULTIPLE-CHOICE QUESTIONS AND ANSWERS

MULTIPLE-CHOICE QUESTIONS

Questions 1–5 are based on the following facts:

A new statute says that "the Administrator of the Environmental Protection Agency shall, by notice-and-comment rulemaking, establish energy efficiency standards for electric appliances and machinery that meet the public interest in energy conservation without harming the economy." The Administrator conducted a notice-and-comment rulemaking establishing new, stricter standards of energy efficiency.

1. Which of the following is an accurate statement of law?

A. This law is unconstitutional because the Administrator can set standards without bicameralism and presentment.
B. This law is unconstitutional because Congress passed the law without notice and comment.
C. This law is valid because the law contains an intelligible principle.
D. This law violates the nondelegation doctrine.

2. Assume during the rulemaking a respected professor of economics submits a comment stating that the Administrator should not increase energy efficiency because this will only cause people to buy more appliances and use more electricity without helping the environment. The Administrator does not respond to this argument in the concise general statement accompanying the rule. The Administrator's action is

A. unlawful because the APA requires that agencies reply to every comment submitted.
B. unlawful because the professor's comment raises an important issue that should have been addressed by the agency.
C. lawful because the professor's argument is not relevant to energy efficiency.
D. lawful because the Administrator used notice-and-comment rulemaking.

3. After the new standards were announced, the Administrator heard complaints from the public and from a Senate committee that the standard was too strict for refrigerators. Ultimately, he amended the standard for refrigerators to make it easier to meet. This action is

A. lawful as long as the Administrator used notice-and-comment rulemaking to amend the standard and the record supports the change.
B. lawful because the issue is committed to the Administrator's discretion by law.
C. unlawful because allowing one legislative committee to establish policy violates *Chadha*.
D. unlawful because the Senators engaged in ex parte comments.

4. Which of the following would be the clearest case for the Administrator's action setting the standards being void?

A. The Administrator made a speech arguing for greater energy conservation while the Administrator was formulating the new standards.
B. The Administrator discussed energy efficiency with the President while the rulemaking for the standards was going on.
C. The Administrator failed to publish notice of the proposed rulemaking in the *Federal Register*.

D. In response to comments, the Administrator slightly decreased the energy efficiency requirements for television sets from what was called for in the original notice.

5. The proper APA standard of judicial review of the Administrator's standards would be

A. arbitrary and capricious because it was an informal rulemaking.
B. substantial evidence because it was a formal rulemaking.
C. de novo because the court should hear new facts.
D. unreviewable because it is committed to agency discretion by law.

Questions 6–8 are based on the following facts:

The U.S. Health and Human Services agency administers a welfare program for poor people and has a rule under which it pays private doctors to provide free health care. After new research proves that most poor people can get free care from private hospitals in the areas in which they live without government payment, the agency conducts a notice-and-comment rulemaking and issues a new rule eliminating free health care provided by the government.

6. Is the agency required to give each recipient a hearing before it terminates the benefit?

A. No, because an advance hearing is never required.
B. No, because the decision is legislative.
C. Yes, because deprivation of a medical benefit can cause a grievous loss.
D. Yes, because the recipients have a property interest in the benefit.

7. Does a doctor who treats many poor people (and receives large government payments) under the program for treating poor people have standing to challenge the new rule on judicial review?

A. No, because the doctor is not injured by the end of the program.
B. Yes, because the doctor is likely within the zone of interests of the welfare program.
C. Yes, because the doctor is the regulated party.
D. Yes, because anyone who disagrees with an agency decision has standing to challenge it.

8. Assume that the federal statute creating the program states that the Department of Health and Human Services of the United States government "shall ensure that welfare recipients are able to procure basic medical care." In the concise general statement, the agency states that it interprets the statutory phrase "shall ensure that recipients are able to procure basic medical care" as allowing the agency to rely on free care by private hospitals. This decision would be reviewed

A. under the arbitrary and capricious test because it is a policy decision.
B. de novo (with attention to the agency's view) because it is a statutory interpretation.
C. under the substantial evidence test because the procedure was formal.
D. under the de novo standard because the agency did not have sufficient facts to make its decision.

9. Which of the following does not describe a form of preemption of state law by federal law?

A. Congress has legislated comprehensively in the area.
B. The area is too important to allow variation from state to state.
C. The state law conflicts with federal law.
D. The state law presents an obstacle to the accomplishment of the goals of the federal law.

10. Because of a parking shortage, the City of Boston decides to close the Boston Common, a large city park, and turn it immediately into a parking lot. You would have standing to sue the city to stop this if

- **A.** you were a resident of Boston.
- **B.** your distinguished ancestor was involved in the planning of Boston Common.
- **C.** you had visited Boston Common in the past.
- **D.** you had visited Boston Common in the past and have definite plans to take your favorite cousin there to ice skate on Frog Pond next winter.

Questions 11–14 are based on the following facts:

The Environmental Protection Agency (EPA) issued a notice of proposed rulemaking stating, "The EPA is looking at a variety of solutions to the problem of gasoline fumes at gasoline stations, especially whether to require a part on every car sold that would capture the fumes and direct them to the car's gas tank. The EPA welcomes comments on any possible solution to this problem." Many comments, including some from automobile makers, showed that a chemical added to gasoline would work better, and the EPA's final rule required the chemical in gasoline, not the part on cars. Oil companies commented favorably to the original proposal but did not address the solution involving the chemical. The oil companies seek judicial review.

11. Which is the best argument that the notice was inadequate?

- **A.** The oil companies could not have reasonably expected the change requiring the chemical in gasoline.
- **B.** The APA requires a second comment period whenever there is any change from the proposal to the final rule.
- **C.** The APA requires that the final rule be included in the notice.
- **D.** The rule is arbitrary and capricious.

12. Which of the following is a good response based on *Vermont Yankee* to the oil companies' challenge?

- **A.** The agency considered the relevant factors and made a reasoned decision.
- **B.** There is substantial evidence to support the rule.
- **C.** The notice satisfied the requirements of the APA's text and a court may not require more.
- **D.** An agency is never required to hold a second comment period because of a change from the proposal to the final rule.

13. Suppose during the comment period an executive of carmaker telephoned the Administrator of the EPA and said, "This proposed rule would cost our company millions of dollars and won't solve the problem. It would work better to put a chemical in gasoline." The Administrator noted the phone call and placed his notes on the public rulemaking record. Did this telephone call violate the APA?

- **A.** No, because ex parte contacts are not prohibited in notice-and-comment rulemaking.
- **B.** No, because the Administrator followed the APA's rules about ex parte contacts.
- **C.** Yes, because the Administrator should not have accepted the telephone call.
- **D.** Yes, because this is an adjudication and ex parte contacts are prohibited by the APA.

14. Suppose an important scientific study of the chemical was contained in a comment that arrived after the end of the comment period and that even though it was late, the EPA considered it, placed it on the public record, and discussed it in the concise general statement. Did the EPA violate the APA?

- **A.** Yes, because opponents did not have a chance to respond to what turned out to be an important comment.
- **B.** Yes, because the rule was arbitrary and capricious.
- **C.** No, because the EPA did not consider the late comment.
- **D.** No, because the APA does not prohibit agencies from considering comments received after the comment period ended.

Questions 15–18 are based on the following facts:

A New York state statute provides: "Public schoolteachers may not be fired without good cause such as poor performance, criminal or immoral conduct, or other conduct harmful to the school system." The principal of a school walks into a classroom after school hours and sees a teacher engaged in sexual contact with a student.

15. The principal suspends the teacher immediately, and schedules a hearing on the teacher's firing for thirty days later. Is this a violation of due process?

- **A.** Yes, because the teacher has a property interest in the job.
- **B.** Yes, because the hearing must come before the suspension.
- **C.** No, because the teacher does not have a property interest in the job.
- **D.** No, because the hearing can be delayed until after the suspension in an emergency.

16. Suppose the teacher argues that, known to the principal, other teachers have had sexual relations with students and have not been fired. Is this a good defense at the hearing?

- **A.** No, because discriminatory enforcement is never a defense.
- **B.** No, because discriminatory enforcement is not a good defense in this case.
- **C.** Yes, because discriminatory enforcement is a good defense whenever the agency cannot show a good reason for enforcing against one violator but not the other.
- **D.** Yes, because this is an abuse of prosecutorial discretion.

17. Suppose that the New York Legislature amends the statute by adding the following language: "Principals may make final decisions on whether to fire public schoolteachers with no judicial review and no hearing." Does this statute mean that teachers may now be fired without hearings?

- **A.** Yes, because the statute says that no hearing is necessary to fire teachers.
- **B.** Yes, because hearings would violate separation of powers.
- **C.** No, because the APA still requires hearings.
- **D.** No, because due process still requires hearings when cause is required to fire teachers.

18. Could New York amend the statute to allow firing teachers without cause?

- **A.** No, because firing without cause always violates due process.
- **B.** No, because the APA requires cause for firing government employees.
- **C.** Yes, because then there would be no property interest.
- **D.** Yes, if each teacher had a hearing before the statue was passed.

19. A statute requires cause for firing the members of the National Labor Relations Board and also for firing the Board's Regional Directors of which there are six across the country. The Board fires the Regional Director for the Southwestern States without cause, and in the firing notice asserts that cause is not necessary. Is the Board correct?

A. No, because Congress may require cause for firing inferior officers.
B. No, because only the President can fire an officer of the United States.
C. Yes, because agency heads can always fire inferior officers.
D. Yes, because the for-cause requirement violates the rule against two levels of for-cause protection.

20. The Census Act orders the Department of Commerce to take a Census every ten years "in such form as prescribed by the Secretary of Commerce." For the 2030 Census, the Secretary decides that the Census will be conducted entirely online with no paper option. Is this decision subject to judicial review?

A. No, because the design of the Census is committed to agency discretion by law.
B. No, because there is no final agency action.
C. Yes, because the provisions and goals of the Census Act provide sufficient guidance for judicial review.
D. Yes, because an accurate Census is very important.

ANSWERS TO MULTIPLE-CHOICE QUESTIONS

1. **C**
2. **B**
3. **A**
4. **C**
5. **A**
6. **B**
7. **B***
8. **B**
9. **B**
10. **D**
11. **A**
12. **C**
13. **A**
14. **A****
15. **D**
16. **B**
17. **D**
18. **C**
19. **D**
20. **C**

* Regarding question 7, there is a good argument that the doctor is not in the zone of interests, that only patients are. However, in recent decades, the courts have loosened up on the zone of interests test and it is likely that the interests of health-care providers were relevant to the establishment of the program.

** Regarding question 14, there is a good argument that D is the correct answer because nothing in the APA addresses the issue of late comments. Most courts would, however, apply the principle in A and require that the comment period be reopened.

Table of Cases

This table includes references to cases cited everywhere in this book, including the exam Q&A sections.

Index

This index includes references to the Capsule Summary and Exam Tips but not to Q&A sections or Flowcharts.

www.ingramcontent.com/pod-product-compliance
Lightning Source LLC
LaVergne TN
LVHW082333200926
848481LV00012B/3337

* 9 7 9 8 8 9 4 1 0 4 7 5 1 *